Word Fugitives

Also by Barbara Wallraff

Word Court

Your Own Words

WORD FUGITIVES

IN PURSUIT OF **WANTED** WORDS

Barbara Wallraff

To Rogers Memorial Library,
With best wishes,

Collins

An Imprint of HarperCollins Publishers

FIRST EDITION

Designed by Ellen Cipriano

Library of Congress Cataloging-in-Publication Data has been filed for.
ISBN-10: 0-06-083273-8

06 07 08 09 10 RRD/WC 10 9 8 7 6 5 4 3 2 1

To my husband, Julian H. Fisher,
who gamely gyred, gimbled, and chortled
along with me all the way through

ACKNOWLEDGMENTS

Many, many thanks to many people: Greg Chaput, for being a wonderful editor; Ellen Cipriano, for getting me to cowboy up; Sam Connery for putting me on to *Burgess Unabridged*; Elizabeth Cox, for giving me a copy of the rarity *Xenia*; Ross Eckler, the editor of *Word Ways*, for, among other assists, sending me copies of neologism-related articles that have run in his journal over the years; Charles Harrington Elster, for turning his considerable mental and bibliographic resources to my purposes on request; the Empress of *The Washington Post*'s Style Invitational column, Pat Myers, for sharing back numbers relating to neologisms and generally being more of a pal than one might expect an Empress would be (the Empress, in turn, would like to graciously acknowledge Russ Beland, "Loser Extraordinaire," for his work in developing an invaluable database of back numbers of The Style Invitational); Diane Aronson Howell, for her skillful book wrangling; Cecilia Hunt, for expertly riding herd on my copy; Alexis Hurley, for her many ideas and her help in rounding up other people's words; Herbert Kleber, M.D., for lending me his *Diagnostic and Statistical Manual of Mental Disorders*, fourth edition; Louis Phillips for sending me "*Mad*'s New Phobias for the '80's"; Steven Pinker, for putting me on to *Sniglets* and *The Deeper Meaning of Liff* back when; Anne Soukhanov, for sharing rare treasures; William Whitworth, for being himself and taking an interest in this book anyway; and Kim Witherspoon, for her excellent agenting.

I am grateful, as well, to my colleagues at *The Atlantic Monthly* who have worked with me on the Word Fugitives columns and Web site; they include Katie Bolick, Benjamin Healy, Emerson Hilton, Michael Kelly, Toby Lester, Amy Meeker, Cullen Murphy, Martha Spaulding, Wen Stephenson, and Eric Westby.

Special thanks go to the eminent and fascinating people who were kind enough to write whole paragraphs of *Word Fugitives* for me: André Bernard, Roy Blount Jr., Emily Cox and Henry Rathvon, Paul Dickson, Faith Eckler, Joseph Epstein, Anne Fadiman, Thierry Fontenelle, Samuel Jay Keyser, Dany Levy, John E. McIntyre, Erin McKean, Allan Metcalf, Dave Morice, Wendalyn Nichols, P. J. O'Rourke (who earns my extra-special gratitude for also giving me, unbidden, his well-thumbed copies of *The Meaning of Liff* and *The Deeper Meaning of Liff*), Patricia C. Post, William A. Sabin, Lloyd Schwartz, Amy Swan, James Trager, and Bill Walsh. Others, too, sent me delightful contributions—but sometimes even the most delicious material must be omitted for the sake of the structure of the work as a whole. Then it becomes a pleasure privately savored by the author together (I hope) with the contributor.

Yet more thanks are due everyone—friends, readers of my columns, and strangers alike—who sent me reports about family words, word fugitives, and fugitives apprehended. With ziraleets and my most spirited xaeulios, I salute you all.

Contents

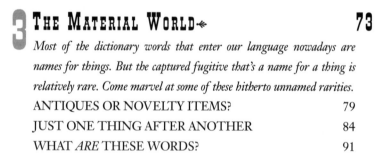

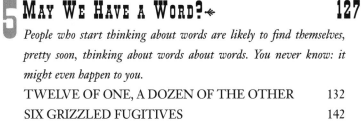

5 MAY WE HAVE A WORD? ← 127

People who start thinking about words are likely to find themselves, pretty soon, thinking about words about words. You never know: it might even happen to you.

6 ODDS AND ENDS ← 155

This is where the word fugitives go if they don't fit into any of the other categories—just so we're clear about what the organizing principle is here.

IN CONCLUSION: KEEPERS 177

What sets a keeper apart from a discard? And do keepers have a future as dictionary words? Sorry, no—this has all been an elaborate fantasy. Here's why.

BIBLIOGRAPHY 189

Word Fugitives

INTRODUCTION: BEFORE THE BEGINNING

Imagine being the first person ever to say anything. What fun it would be to fill in the world with words: *tree, dog, wolf, fire, husband, wife, kiddies.* But putting names to things quickly gets complicated. For instance, if I call my husband *husband*, what should I call my friend's husband? Just for the sake of argument, let's say he's a *man.* So is my husband still my *husband*, or is he, too, a *man*? Or maybe he could go by both names. If we let him have more than one name, he can also be a *father*—and a *hunter-gatherer.*

And, say! Let's make up words for actions, as well as things: The tree *grows* new leaves. The dog *runs*—he runs *away from* the wolf and *toward* the fire. You know what? This pastime has possibilities.

All right, I'm sure it wasn't literally like that. But before the beginning, there weren't any words. And now, obviously, there are millions of them, in thousands of languages. Our own language, if we count all the terms in all the specialized jargons attached to English, has millions of words. Between prehistory and the present came a long period in which people who didn't know a word for something usually had no way of finding out whether any such word already existed. For example, suppose you wanted to know a plant's name—maybe the name of a particular one that could be used medicinally as a sedative but could also be lethal in high doses. If you asked around and nobody knew what it was called, you'd have little choice but to make up a name. Let's say *hemlock*. Why *hemlock* and not some other word? Nobody knows anymore. The *Oxford English Dictionary* says *hemlock* is "of obscure origin: no cognate word is found in the other lang[uage]s."

William Shakespeare lived and wrote during that long, linguistically benighted period. Nonetheless, he managed to express himself pretty well in writing. Shakespeare is thought to have been a prolific word coiner. *Besmirch, impede, rant,* and *wild-goose chase* are a few of the more than a thousand words and phrases that he evidently added to our language. His coinages tend to be more a matter of tinkering or redefining than of plucking words out of thin air (or *ayre*, as Shakespeake spelled the word in the phrase *into thin air*, in *The Tempest*). For instance, *smirch* was a verb before Shakespeare added the prefix *be-* to it. *Impediment*, derived from Latin, was in use in English for at least two hundred years before

Shakespeare came up with *impede*. But as scholars of Shakespearean English acknowledge, only a limited amount of writing survives from Shakespeare's day apart from his own. Many words whose first recorded use appears in one of Shakespeare's plays may have been familiar to Elizabethan-era conversationalists. Or maybe in conversation Shakespeare coined many more words than we know—but because he didn't write them down, they've been lost to history.

The English language kept swallowing up, digesting, and drawing energy from other languages' words. As English grew, word lists of various kinds were compiled and circulated. For instance, there were lists of "terms of venery"—words of the kind ("a *pride* of lions," "a *murder* of crows," "a *gam* of whales") in which *An Exaltation of Larks*, by James Lipton, has latterly specialized. The earliest still in existence, *The Egerton Manuscript*, dates back to about 1450. *The Book of St. Albans*, "the most complete and important of the early lists," according to *An Exaltation of Larks*, appeared in 1486. The ambitions of language reference works continued to grow. The first comprehensive English dictionary, compiled by Nathan Bailey, was published in Britain in 1730. The word *copyright* hadn't yet been coined. Samuel Johnson did a bit of cribbing from Bailey to create his famous dictionary of 1755—by which time *copyright* was indeed in use. Still, it took about another half century for the word to make its way into Johnson's dictionary.

In America in 1783, a twenty-five-year-old Noah Webster began publishing "spelling books." *Webster's Spelling Book* sold more than a million copies annually for years—an astonishing number considering that in 1790, according to the first U.S. census, the total U.S. population was less than four million. Far from resting on his laurels, Webster kept working away until he had finished his masterwork, the two-volume *American Dictionary of the English Language*, published in 1828. From then on out, Americans as well as Britons had fewer excuses to invent words.

Of course, coining words to meet real needs continued—and it continues, especially in specialized realms like medicine, technology, fashion, cooking, cartooning, online games, and so on. The world contains many specialized realms. Sometimes what constitutes a need for a term is subjective. Why do we need *myocardial infarction* when we already have *heart attack*? Physicians think we do. Why do we need *bling-bling* when we already have *flashy jewelry*? Movie stars and rap musicians think we do. Well, jargon and slang have been with us a long time. New words coined to meet needs—objective or subjective, real or perceived—have been with us since the beginning. The impulse to coin words today may well be a vestige of the impulse that gave humankind language in the first place.

Jargon, slang, and words coined in all seriousness are not, however, our subject in this book. If a word is known to hundreds or thousands of people, most of whom take knowing it as a sign of kinship with one another, and very few of whom believe they invented it, then for our purposes it is a domesticated word, a dictionary word, as opposed to a captured fugitive. The distinction between domesticated words and captured fugitives is a blurry one, for sure. Some words that have been domesticated thoroughly enough to appear in dictionaries deserve, in my opinion, to be let go—say, *funplex*, *carbs*, and the verb *gift*. (You probably have your own, longer list.) Such words should be allowed to scuttle back to wherever they came from. On the other hand, some eagerly sought fugitives have eluded capture for decades or even centuries—for instance, a grammatical *and* idiomatic word to use in questions instead of "*Aren't* I" (ungrammatical) or "*Am* I *not*" (stilted), and a gender-neutral singular pronoun that could take over from *he or she*.

★ ★ ★

What exactly is a "word fugitive"? Simply put, it's a word that someone is looking for, which other people helpfully try to find or coin. To explain the idea more cosmically, if words are conceptual matter, word fugitives are conceptual anti-matter. Word fugitives are holes in the language that dictionary words have failed to fill. *Tree*, *dog*, *wolf*, *grow*, *run*, and the many thousands of other words that we can look up are all well and good; they've long served us admirably. But time marches on, and now, in the twenty-first century, wouldn't it be handy to have a word for the momentary confusion people experience when they hear a cell phone ringing and wonder whether it's theirs? Those of us who've left our caveman past behind might get more everyday use out of a word like that than we do out of words like *cudgel*, *snare*, and *leg-hold trap*. The squeamish among us, highly civilized beings that we have become, might even appreciate being able to put a name to the fear of running over squirrels.

And, for once, we can get what we want. Word coining seems to be ingrained in each of us. Linguists have determined that children don't simply hear and remember all the forms of all the words that enter their vocabulary. As soon as children are familiar with a pattern like *I smile, my father smiles, I smiled, my father smiled*, they easily generate *I run, my father runs, I runned, my father runned*. They half-hear things and in response coin charming words like *rainbrella* and *lasterday*. Until children learn their irregular verbs and acquire a big, all-purpose vocabulary, they're very good at spontaneously filling holes in their language. Scientists have reported that about 40 percent of twins under the age of five or six (and some close-in-age siblings too) have a private language they speak only with each other. Surely at least that high a proportion of families have a few words of private language they use among themselves.

Some "family words" are, more or less, souvenirs of the family's experiences. Other family words exist to fill holes in the standard vocabulary—sometimes holes that many other families have separately noticed and filled. Lots of people, it turns out, call nephews and nieces collectively *niblings* or *nieblings* or *nieflings*. I've heard from or read about dozens of them. Many of these people believe they or someone they know coined their word. Evidently, *niblings*, *nieblings*, and *nieflings* are coined again and again. But because they rarely break out of the spoken language into print, they haven't made it into our dictionaries. Thus family words make up a half-hidden level of language.

The conceptual matter of family words, like that of other kinds of words, has anti-matter, or word fugitives: meanings for which we'd all like to have words, and for which people keep coining words. What word, for example, describes a grown-up's "boyfriend" or "girlfriend"? In cold climates, what might we call the grubby lumps of ex-snow that cars track into our driveways and garages? In the case of each of these word fugitives—and others—many possibilities have been floated, but none has caught the fancy of a critical mass of English-speakers. So people just keep asking why there's no word with that meaning and trying to come up with one.

★ ★ ★

Credit for being the first to neologize publicly on purpose is usually given to two Englishmen, Lewis Carroll and Edward Lear, for their "nonsense verse." " 'Twas brillig and the slithy toves / Did gyre and gimble in the wabe," Carroll wrote, in his poem "Jabberwocky," published in *Through the Looking Glass*, in 1872. *Brillig*? *Slithy*? *Gyre*? *Gimble*? *Wabe*? Carroll (whose non–nom de plume was Charles Lutwidge Dodgson) coined them all.

Lear wrote, in 1867: "The Owl and the Pussy-cat went to sea / In a beautiful pea-green boat, / . . . / They dined on mince, and slices of quince, / Which they ate with a runcible spoon." Behold the world's first use of *runcible spoon*. And what does it refer to? According to the *Oxford English Dictionary*, the term "in later use applied to a kind of fork used for pickles, etc., curved like a spoon and having three broad prongs of which one has a sharp edge." But, the *OED* notes, "the illustrations provided by Lear himself for his books of verse give no warrant for this later interpretation."

Though many "nonsense" words might seem arbitrary—can you guess from looking at *brillig* or *runcible* what it means?—a number of Lewis Carroll's coinages have a special property. Humpty Dumpty explains this to Alice a bit further on in *Through the Looking Glass*, when she asks for his help with the unfamiliar words in "Jabberwocky":

> " 'BRILLIG' means four o'clock in the afternoon—the time when you begin BROILING things for dinner."
>
> "That'll do very well," said Alice; "and 'SLITHY'?"
>
> "Well, 'SLITHY' means 'lithe and slimy.' 'Lithe' is the same as 'active.' You see it's like a portmanteau—there are two meanings packed up into one word."

Portmanteau words—eureka! With this idea, Carroll bestowed a versatile gift on the world of recreational neologizing.

Because portmanteau words are derived from dictionary words, they tend to be less opaque than other new coinages. In fact, *chortle*, another portmanteau word that Carroll coined in "Jabberwocky," became a dictionary word, because people readily understood how to use it. The *Oxford English Dictionary* explains its roots like this: "app[arently] with some suggestion of *chuckle*, and of *snort*." Unfortunately, a portmanteau itself ("a large leather suitcase that opens into two hinged compartments," as the *American Heritage Dictionary* defines it) has by now become the kind of thing found only in museums and antique shops. It's probably time to hunt up a less anachronistic term to carry the meaning into the future.

Although we owe a debt to Carroll and Lear, what they did is not recreational word coining of the kind that this book is mainly about. Carroll and Lear invented their words for literary purposes—much as Shakespeare did. Literary figures from James Joyce (*bababadalgharaghtakamminarronnkonnbronntonnerronntuonnthunntrovarrhounawnskawntoohoohoordenenthurnuk!*) and George Orwell (*Newspeak*) to J.R.R. Tolkien (*hobbit*) and J.K. Rowling (*quidditch*) have intentionally made up words the better to convey worlds largely of their invention. "Recreational word coining," as the phrase is more often used in this book, describes odd corners of the world we know.

"Recreational redefining" also describes the world we know and is part of *Word Fugitives'* purview. Therefore, before we get acquainted with the first true recreational word coiner, who came a bit later, let's meet the pioneer on this linguistic front—the American writer Ambrose Bierce. Bierce was a near contemporary of Carroll's and Lear's. In 1875 he finished a freelance manuscript that included forty-eight English words and his redefinitions of them. This, the first sulfurous spark of what would become *The Devil's Dictionary*, failed to set the world on fire. Six years later, Bierce was named editor of a new satirical journal, *Wasp*, and he immediately began writing and publishing a feature that offered "twisty new definitions of shopworn old words," as Roy Morris Jr. explains in his introduction to the current Oxford edition of *The Devil's Dictionary*. Many of the words from *Wasp* also took their place among the 998 redefined words that ultimately made up Bierce's best-known book. In 1912, not long before Bierce lit out for Mexico and from there disappeared off the face of the earth, he published twelve volumes of his *Collected Works*, including *The Devil's Dictionary*. An *admiral*, he wrote, is "that part of a war-ship which does the talking while the figure-head does the thinking." A *habit* is "a shackle for the free." *Zeal* is "a certain nervous disorder afflicting the young and inexperienced. A passion that goeth before a sprawl." Since 1912, *The Devil's Dictionary* has never been out of print.

As for the first true recreational word coiner, he was another American: Gelett Burgess. Like Carroll and Lear in England, Burgess published nonsense verse—one of his claims to fame is the poem "The Purple Cow." More to the point, in 1914 he published a spurious dictionary, *Burgess Unabridged: A Dictionary of Words You Have Always Needed*. Among the words in it is *blurb*— another of Burgess's claims to fame, for this creation of his remains in use, still with roughly the meaning he assigned it. Alas, few of his other words ever caught on. You will, nonetheless, have a chance to get to know some of them in this book.

That Burgess really was up to something new in *Burgess Unabridged* becomes clear when it is compared with a little unsigned piece that pre-dates Burgess's dictionary by six years. Titled "Improvised Words," it appeared in *The Atlantic Monthly* in 1908. Its author whimsically proposed to "write an addendum for my dictionary, have it neatly typewritten, and paste it right after the Z's, but before the Foreign and Abbreviated Phrases." Then he or she went on to discuss an assortment of nine coined or redefined words. For instance: "There is hardly a family but has some expressive improvised word. In my own family *humbly* reigns supreme. This is not the adverb of current usage, but an adjective, and a cross between *humble* and *homely*; and it was used to describe our washwoman. . . ." Some of the other words covered were dialect. For instance: a "good Pennsylvania word, and very full of meaning, is to *neb*, signifying 'to pry, to thrust one's self in where one is not needed and not wanted, to mix into other people's affairs.'" The late-twentieth-century *Dictionary of American Regional English* confirms that indeed this is a Pennsylvania word having that meaning.

"Improvised Words" shows, in part, that as far back as a century ago, the use of terms that were not in the dictionary was considered worthy of comment. It also shows, by jumbling together family words, regional dialect, and other kinds of non-dictionary words, how vague—or naive—people at the time tended to be in their thinking about non-dictionary words.

During and between the two world wars, fine English-speaking minds seem to have been occupied by things other than coining words for the heck of it. At least, to judge by the number of books published on the subject, recreational coining went through a lull. But it came roaring back in the mid to late twentieth century. Over the past few decades in particular, coining and redefining has taken many forms. I won't describe them all here—please see the bibliography for an expanded list of sources—but I will touch on some highlights.

An Exaltation of Larks, the collection of venerable terms of venery, originally appeared in 1968 and has stayed in print through several revisions. In the *Ultimate Edition*, published in 1991, well over half the pages are devoted to terms that the author, James Lipton (now better known as the host of *Inside the Actors Studio*, on the Bravo channel), either coined himself or found in the work of contemporary writers: "a *phalanx* of flashers," Kurt Vonnegut; "a *mews* of cathouses," Neil Simon; "an *om* of Buddhists," George Plimpton.

A new twist came in 1983, with the publication of *The Mean-*

ing of Liff, by the British writers Douglas Adams (the author of the 1979 best seller *The Hitchhiker's Guide to the Galaxy*) and John Lloyd. The book's preface reads:

> In Life,* there are many hundreds of common experiences, feelings, situations and even objects which we all know and recognize, but for which no words exist.
>
> On the other hand, the world is littered with thousands of spare words which spend their time doing nothing but loafing about on signposts pointing at places.
>
> Our job, as we see it, is to get these words down off the signposts and into the mouths of babes and sucklings and so on, where they can start earning their keep in everyday conversation and make a more positive contribution to society.
>
> *And, indeed, in Liff.

And so *Liff,* the name of a suburb of Dundee, Scotland, took on a new meaning; it was defined as "a book the contents of which are totally belied by its cover. For instance, any book the dust jacket of which bears the words 'This book will change your life.'" (How did you guess? *The Meaning of Liff'*s dust jacket bore those very words.)

Adams and Lloyd merrily misappropriated geographic names from *Aasleagh* ("a liqueur made only for drinking at the end of a revoltingly long bottle party when all the drinkable drink has been drunk") to *Zeal Monachorum* ("[skiing term] To ski with *zeal monachorum* is to descend the top three quarters of the mountain in a quivering blue funk, but on arriving at the gentle bit just in front of the restaurant to whiz to a stop like a victorious slalom champion"). Seven years later Adams and Lloyd published an expanded edition, *The Deeper Meaning of Liff*, which included many new place-names and definitions for them. Most of the ones from the original book remained the same, though this time *Liff* itself was defined as "a common object or experience for which no word yet exists."

In the meantime, *sniglets* had been giving Liffs some stiff competition. Rich Hall, a writer and cast member on HBO's comedy show *Not Necessarily the News* (which, some say, was patterned on the British program *Not the Nine O'Clock News*, for which Douglas Adams's co-author, John Lloyd, was the producer), came up with the idea of a *sniglet* as "any word that doesn't appear in the dictionary, but should." *Liff* and *sniglet*, that is, are almost synonyms. (And, again, a *word fugitive* is not their antonym but their antimatter: the idea for a word missing from our language.) Sniglets fans sent Rich Hall words like *aquadextrous*, "possessing the ability to turn the bathtub faucet on and off with your toes," and *profanitype*, "the special symbols used by cartoonists to replace swear words (points, asterisks, stars, and so on)." The coinages were regularly featured on the TV show and collected in a series of five paperbacks.

Next came a more serious and high-minded variation on the theme. The writer Jack Hitt asked a number of writers and artists "if they had ever had the experience of running across a meaning for which there is no word," and he turned the words they proposed into a piece published in *Harper's Magazine* in 1990. This was so well received that Hitt expanded the article into a 1992 book, *In a Word*. The letter Hitt sent to potential contributors to the book explained his goal like this: "What I am trying to create is an actual dictionary of meanings that need words in our language. I am not asking for silly coinages, funny jargon, or useless meanings. That is not to suggest that your meaning and its word can't be funny. I am simply trying to wave off any attempts at sniglets."

Paul Dickson pursued non-dictionary words from yet another angle in his 1998 book *Family Words*. His focus was "linguistic curiosit[ies] . . . understood by a very small circle." He explained: "When you say that word outside the family or small group of friends, others don't know what you're talking about. More often than not, family words can be traced back to a kid or a grandparent, and sometimes they get passed down from generation to generation." Some family words that Dickson collected are cute; some are droll; some, as Dickson noted, keep being coined again and again; and these categories overlap.

And then there's *The Washington Post's* Style Invitational contest, which has been running every week for thirteen years. Under the control of "Czar" Gene Weingarten until 2003 and now under "Empress" Pat Myers, The Style Invitational issues clever verbal challenges of many kinds. Sometimes the week's contest has to do with neologizing or redefining existing words—and the results are always hilarious. The Style Invitational—along with a column by Bob Levey that included a separate neologism contest once a month from 1983 until Levey's retirement in 2004—has made *The Washington Post* America's paper of recreational-word-coining record.

Another variation on the theme: from 1999 to 2002, *This Morning*, a Canadian Broadcasting Corporation radio show, instituted a weekly sniglets-like feature called Wanted Words. Its highlights are captured in two books, *Wanted Words* (2000) and *Wanted Words 2* (2001), both edited by Jane Farrow, whose brainchild the radio segments were.

Throughout this book, these and other sources of coinages and redefinitions will repeatedly cross your path. Because I quote from a variety of sources, which identify the coiners of their words in various ways, the way I identify coiners will, regrettably, be inconsistent and sometimes seemingly incomplete. I have, though, taken the liberty of imposing consistency on the formats—italic, for instance—of words from all sources, and done a bit of light copy-editing, to eliminate trivial inconsistencies. Archaic, rare, and dialectal dictionary words from various sources will crop up too. These are intended to demonstrate that words which once occupied a secure place in our language can be indistinguishable from even the most frivolous neologisms.

★ ★ ★

Where do word fugitives fit in this taxonomy? Why, they stand on the shoulders of the giants of recreational word coining. From this vantage point, word fugitives survey the present and peer into the future.

When I came up with them, I was innocent of the tradition that they would carry on. In fact, I stumbled into the field of recreational word coining by accident. Since 1995 I've published a column, Word Court, in *The Atlantic Monthly*, in which I rule on readers' language disputes and answer their language questions. In 1997 or 1998, as fodder for Word Court, someone sent me this:

> Here's my question, which my mother and I have been wondering about for years: When you dig a hole in the ground with a shovel, and pile the excavated earth next to the hole, you stand on the ground between the hole and the pile. Is there a name for the area or piece of ground that you are standing on between the nascent hole and the growing pile? We thought up *holeside* but are hoping you can give us more informed and authoritative information.

Now, never mind that this letter reads like a verbal version of a What's wrong with this picture? puzzle. (You and your *mother* have been wondering about that? For *years*? Etc.) And never mind what suggestions others eventually came up with for the word; they got the job done but were not gloriously inspired. I was hooked, dazzled even—as you can see.

A few more "Is there a word for . . ." questions trickled in, and I began to think it would be fun to include a group of them in a book I was writing based on Word Court. I asked *The Atlantic*'s Web-site staff to help me gather some more, and together we came up with the interactive Web feature "Word Fugitives: America's Most Wanted Words." Long after *Word Court*, the book, was published, the Web site continued to run "Word Fugitives," because it remained popular. Then I began publishing Word Fugitives as a column in *The Atlantic*, alternating it with Word Court. Now it's Word Fugitives' turn to be a book.

Please note that the sections that may look as if they're lifted from the magazine column are not simply that. I've modified nearly all the discussions of people's responses to questions—some subtly, some thoroughly. And I've included new questions for which I've found answers in other sources. What's more, the parts of a tightly structured magazine page, which always presents two new word fugitives and discusses two old ones, have been fitted together into a whole larger than the sum of. This whole allows us, here, to indulge in meta-considerations.

For instance, can we hope that any of the words we craft will enter the standard vocabulary? Are we following in Shakespeare's footsteps—even if only stumblingly? Are we at least on the same path as the futurologist Faith Popcorn, whose 1986 coinage *cocoon-*

ing (meaning "enveloping oneself in comforts and staying home") now appears in several standard dictionaries? Not to be a spoiler, but no, unfortunately, we are neither Shakespeare nor Popcorn—as I will explain in the book's conclusion.

Another meta-question: What kinds of neologisms pop into many people's heads simultaneously? Throughout the book, I'll tell you what were especially popular responses to fugitives questions. But I'll pass along plenty of idiosyncratic responses too. It's fascinating to see how different people's minds work.

And what kinds of neologisms pop into many people's heads as answers to diverse word-fugitives questions? A tiny hint: If you're tempted to play Word Fugitives as a game with your family or friends, please deduct half a point—or knock off a full point, or salute the coiner with a Bronx cheer—for any coinage that's a twist on *premature ejaculation* or *coitus interruptus*. If you can't imagine why I say that (and I have a reason beyond the blindingly obvious one of good taste), this, too, will be explained in the conclusion.

Yet another: What kinds of words do people tend to want? Does this say anything about us as a society—or at least as a self-selected set of word-game players? Make of it what you will, but when I started shuffling through years' worth of *The Atlantic*'s Word Fugitives, it seemed to me that they easily sorted themselves out as follows.

Many people ask for words to describe previously uncharted expanses of our inner worlds; their requests, together with responses to those requests, appear in Chapter One. Other people want words for *other* people—people they can't relate to and don't want to; that's Chapter Two. Over the years I've gotten surprisingly few requests for names for things; so Chapter Three, though it's titled "The Material World," is at least as much about our relationship to things as it is about things themselves.

And then, what would modern life be without petty irritations? You'll find a compendium of such things in Chapter Four. Chapter Five consists of requests for words about words; people who enjoy word fugitives seem to be more likely than average to have words on their minds. Chapter Six is filled with those holdouts that resist categorization; it's the hall closet where miscellaneous stuff is stashed, the junk drawer in the kitchen, the "Pick a Surprise!" basket at the jumble sale.

Along the way are diversions, digressions, and pop quizzes—sidebars, we publishing insiders call them. And as you'll see, each chapter also includes a bit of commentary from friends or friends of friends, mostly workers in words—writers, editors, crossword-puzzle constructors, designers, booksellers, lexicographers, publishers. These people have not only targeted a word fugitive or two but also captured it or them. Finally, each chapter includes pleas for help from people whose fugitives are still at large. Fugitives eluding capture are everywhere. Will you do your bit to round some of them up and bring them in?

★　★　★

Before we get into any of that, though, may I tell you the way I hope you'll read this book?

Slowly.

In the Q&A-type sections of the book where the word fugitives themselves appear, I've intentionally not put my favorite response in huge type right after the request that elicited it. This is partly to give you the chance to think up words of your own before you see the clever ones other people have coined. And it's partly because the more slowly you go—the more time you spend reflecting on the myriad possibilities our language affords us—the more opportunity this book will have to mess with your head.

Maybe English seems to you now like an orderly array of components that you can use to assemble any idea, concept, thought, or eidolon (*eidolon*? see Chapter One) that comes to mind; maybe it seems like a great big set of verbal Lego blocks. But, I submit, it's really more like a secondhand store or junkyard full of sturdy, versatile tools; battered old implements that have been put to a succession of uses; strange objects that never have fulfilled any purpose very well; anachronisms that have been retrofitted with new parts to suit contemporary requirements; and shiny castoff novelties. Sometimes when you're searching for a word that means just what you want it to, you won't find anything suitable anywhere and you'll have to patch together your own out of bits and scraps.

When I began working on the book, I sought out as many as possible living creators of sources from which I'll be quoting. Maybe they had a word or two they didn't know what to do with anymore? I wrote them to say I'd be honored to include those words in *Word Fugitives*. Understandably enough, none of them sent me new words, though some of them pointed me toward earlier neologizing of theirs that I hadn't discovered on my own. As for those friends and friends of friends I prevailed on, I told them that the words I was particularly eager for would be "light-hearted and timeless." I asked for "witty words that readers might enjoy using with friends." You be the judge of how well everyone followed instructions as you read the responses they sent me. In fact, a few of those responses seem to belong right here.

RUSTLED UP

The cruciverbalists, or crossword-puzzle construc-tors, Emily Cox and Henry Rathvon wrote me:

Crossword writers invent neologisms habitually, but these coinages tend to be in the limited service of thematic puns. For example, a puzzle purporting to feature new sorts of doctors might include a *cairopractor* (an Egyptian expert on posture), a *fizzician* (a dispenser of carbonated remedies), and a *dormatologist* (a medic for college students). Such clowning around is typical of crossword makers, and is one of the happy perks (or irksome obsessions, depending on your point of view) of the puz biz. But even when we've put our crossword toys away, we tend to be word-benders. If we have a brainstorm, we're liable to call it a *psychlone*. For us, the line between real and invented words is arbitrary.

Joseph Epstein, a noted essayist and a former editor of *The American Scholar*, wrote me:

In a letter to Louise Colet, his mistress, Flaubert writes that the words do not exist to give full expression to his love for her. "The language," he writes, "is inept." I, too, have found the language frequently inept, and thus have had to fall back on inventing words the language ought to supply but doesn't.

Paul Valéry says somewhere that there ought to be a word to describe the condition between talent and genius. I think he's right. I also think there must be hundreds of other such words that await invention.

One word I have devised that I should like to see in a future dictionary of neologisms (edited by Barbara Wallraff) is *virtucrat*, for those people whose sense of their own high virtue derives from their nauseatingly enlightened political opinions. I first used this word in an article of many moons ago in *The New York Times Magazine*. I'm pleased to note that *virtucrat* is slowly making its way into the language, and I see it pop up from time to time—sometimes spelled *virtuecrat*—in other people's scribblings, and not always with the precise meaning I intended for it to have.

And Erin McKean, editor in chief of U.S. dictionaries for the Oxford University Press, wrote me:

I use words that aren't in dictionaries all the time. Dictionaries are sadly finite—if they recorded every nonce word, one-off metaphorical extension, and verb-or-noun-ification (like *verb-or-noun-ification*), lexicographers would be even more harried, overwhelmed, and distracted than they already are. I also use undictionaried words for the pure fun of it, and because I can.

Often people I am talking to apologize for using words that aren't in the dictionary. I wish they wouldn't—apologize, that is. If people restricted themselves to using only what the dictionary-makers have already caught and tagged, I'd soon be out of work, and English would stagnate.

★ ★ ★

So here we have longtime word professionals of assorted stripes admitting (cheerfully!) to using non-dictionary words. If they can do it, so can we all.

OUR UNRULY INNER LIVES

In a sense, this whole book is about our unruly inner lives. Language, some linguists say, organizes experience. But language itself is hideously disorganized—or at any rate, the English language is. Sometimes we have plenty of synonyms or near-synonyms to choose from—for instance, *idea, concept, thought, inspiration, notion, surmise, theory, impression, perception, observation, mental picture.* More specialized meanings get specialized words. If, say, you're looking for a word that can mean either "a phantom" or "an ideal"—why, *eidolon* stands ready to serve. And yet some fairly common things and phenomena remain nameless. For instance, what would you call the experience of having recently heard about something for the first time and then starting to notice it everywhere?

That particular word fugitive (which you'll find captured and discussed shortly) is worthy of note, because once you're aware of it, if you begin rooting around in coined words, you'll find it popping up maybe not everywhere but certainly hither and yon. Essentially the same question is asked by the writer Lia Matera in the book *In a Word*; Matera suggests we call the experience *toujours vu*. Another book, *Wanted Words 2*, asks the question, too, and presents more than a dozen possible answers, including *newbiquitous* and *coincidensity*. Are *toujours vu*, *newbiquitous*, and *coincidensity* really words? No, not quite. They are the verbal equivalents of trees that fall soundlessly if no one is listening. They are Tinker Bell, whose little light will be extinguished if we don't believe in her. They are words only if we use them.

See how unruly we've managed to get already?

It's only going to get worse—especially if you didn't read the Introduction. We're about to delve into questions that people have posed and answers that others—kind, clever souls—have proposed, and there will be digressions along the way. If you find yourself wondering, What's up with that? turn back! You are worthy, of course, but not fully prepared for the journey ahead.

U

"What's the word for that restless feeling that causes me to repeatedly peer into the refrigerator when I'm bored? There's nothing to do in there."

—Nick Fedoroff, Wilmington, N.C.

Robert Clark, of Austin, Texas, is someone who knows this feeling. He wrote: "I often find myself revisiting the same refrigerator I left in disappointment only moments ago, as if this time the perfect snack—which I somehow managed to overlook before—will be there waiting for me. Almost invariably I find that I am suffering from a *leftoveractive imagination*."

Cold comfort, refrigerator magnetism, smorgasboredom, and *freonnui* are all coinages that lots of people suggested. Other ideas include *stirvation* (Jon Craig, of Del Rey Oaks, Calif.) and *procrastifrigeration* (Jared Paventi, of Liverpool, N.Y.). A person in the relevant frame of mind, says Dick Bruno, of Hackensack, N.J., is *bored chilly*. And Chris Rooney, of San Francisco, wrote, "Back in my bachelor days, when I wasn't going out with someone that night I'd head to the fridge for some *expiration dating*."

Then there were the brand-specific coinages, such as "the urge to *play tag with the Maytag*" (Marcel Couturier, of Nashua,

N.H.); *Frigistaire* (Bob Segal, of Chicago, among others); and the upscale *Sub-Zero interest* (Daniel Markovitz, of New York City).

But these are getting much too fancy, don't you think? Let's go with the neat, uncomplicated coinage **fridgety**, submitted by many people including Allan Crossman, of Oakland, Calif., who submitted it first.

U

"I'm looking for a term that describes the momentary confusion experienced by everyone in the vicinity when a cell phone rings and no one is sure if it is his/hers or not."

—Allison A. Johnson, Glendale, Calif.

You might call that *conphonesion* (Paul Holman, of Austin, Texas), *phonundrum* (Pam Blanco, of Warwick, R.I.), or *ringchronicity* (Alan Tobey, of Berkeley, Calif.). Or what about *ringmarole* (Jim Hutt, of Blue Mountain Lake, N.Y.), *ringxiety* (William A. Browne Jr., of Indianapolis), or *fauxcellarm* (Gordon Wilkinson, of Mill Bay, British Columbia)?

But maybe this confusion is best described as **pandephonium**—as Michael W. Pajak, of Portland, Maine, was the first among several to suggest.

U

"Here's a phenomenon that cries out for a word to describe it: the state of being amused (irrationally so, it seems to me) by the antics of one's pets."

—Kevin Taylor, Boise, Idaho

The possibilities include "*petaphilia* or *pestaphilia*—depending on your perspective," according to Jim Ennis, of Huntsville, Ala. "I suppose if I had a bird, it might make me *raptorous*. However, in reality I am *catatonic*," wrote Denny Stein, of Baltimore. And Glenn Werner, of Pine Bush, N.Y., wrote, "When one gets particularly engrossed with one's pet, especially in the presence of others, it's called being *petantic*."

An especially frolicsome invention is ***fur-shlugginer*** (coined by Jason Taniguchi and his fellow members of the erstwhile Toronto, Ontario, Serial Diners Collective [don't ask]). Those who have never been regular readers of *Mad* magazine may be interested to learn that this is a variant on a pseudo-Yiddish word that in Alfred E. Neuman's lexicon means "crazy."

Incidentally, the very existence of the monosyllabic and generic word *pet* implies that English is already way ahead of other languages in the domestic-fauna department. Speakers of Romance languages must resort to phrases like *animale prediletto* and *animal de estimação* to get the same idea across.

U

"I'd like a word for that feeling that you always arrive after the heyday, the boom, or the free ride. For example, when I started college, the drinking age was raised; when I graduated from law school, the job market disappeared. Now I am trying to buy a house, and prices are soaring. This is more than disappointment. It's about missing a departure when you've never been advised of the schedule."

—Catherine Mehno, Weehawken, N.J.

More than a few people thinking about this word fugitive make a generational association, and take the matter personally. For instance, Yvonne deReynier, of Seattle, admitted, "It's a feeling I'm familiar with myself," and suggested the term *GenXasperation*. Popular suggestions of the same type include *buster* and *late boomer*.

General-purpose coinages include *fate and switch* (Andrea Ball, of Chapel Hill, N.C.), *latedown* (Dennis Harbaugh, of Waterloo, Iowa), *missappointment* (an oft-repeated suggestion), *serendiplash* (Margaret Swanson, of Chatham, Mass.), and *unjust in time* (T. H. Arnold, of Cambridge, Mass.).

"There has long been an idiomatic expression to describe this

A ROUNDUP OF FUGITIVES

Can you match the definitions with the words people have coined for them? The matchups, together with the sources of these words, appear on the next page.

1. The act of entering a room and forgetting why   *Aberystwyth*

2. All excited at suddenly remembering a wonderful piece of gossip that you want to pass on to somebody   *Anticippointment*

3. Confidence in the kitchen   *Berumptotfreude*

4. A feeling of great anticipation coupled with the knowledge that what is anticipated—for instance, a movie sequel—will not live up to expectations   *Cooksure*

5. Having a secret urge to expedite the person ahead of you through a revolving door   *Destinesia*

6. Having so many choices that you take forever to make up your mind   *Galubcious*

7. The internalized voices of relatives; that inescapable ancestral drone of commentary and judgment   *Hygog*

8. Lurid thrills derived from the deaths of celebrities   *Kinnitus*

9. A nostalgic yearning that is in itself more pleasant than the thing being yearned for   *Malaybalay*

10. The sensation of the tongue wrapping itself around the first mouthful of a chocolate dessert covered with whipped cream   *Menuitis*

11. State of euphoria reached when scratching any itch   *Pushopathic*

12. An unsatisfied desire, something out of one's reach   *Scratchtasy*

FUGITIVE NO MORE

Here's what was coined, and where.[*]

1. **Destinesia** is the word for forgetting why one has entered a room, according to *Angry Young Sniglets*.
2. Being excited at remembering gossip is called **Malaybalay** in *The Deeper Meaning of Liff*. Elsewhere, *Malaybalay* is the name of a land-locked city in the southern Philippines.
3. To be **cooksure** is to have culinary confidence, according to *Not the Webster's Dictionary*—which, by the way, is definitely not a dictionary.
4. **Anticippointment** is looking forward to something you know won't live up to expectations, according to Lanora Hurley, manager of a Harry W. Schwartz Bookshop in Milwaukee.
5. The **pushopathic** have that secret urge triggered by a revolving door and another person, according to *Angry Young Sniglets*.
6. **Menuitis** is used by Shari Gackstatter's family, in New Cumberland, Pa., to mean having too many choices, according to *Family Words*.
7. **Kinnitus** describes relatives' internalized voices, according to the writer Ellen Gruber Garvey, in *In a Word*.
8. **Berumptotfreude** refers to lurid thrills one gets from the deaths of celebrities. For *In a Word*, the writer Douglas Coupland derived it from the German words for "famous," "dead," and "happy."
9. **Aberystwyth** is a nostalgic yearning, according to *The Deeper Meaning of Liff*. It is otherwise a university town on the coast of Wales.
10. According to the actress Katharine Hepburn, in *In a Word*, the first mouthful of chocolate and whipped cream is **galubcious**.
11. **Scratchtasy** is, of course, itch-scratching euphoria. The word appears in *When Sniglets Ruled the Earth*.
12. Gelett Burgess called an unsatisfied desire a **hygog** in his 1914 book *Burgess Unabridged*. He didn't explain why.

[*]Please see the Bibliography, on page 189, for complete information about the sources given here and throughout the book.

feeling: *missing the boat*," wrote Lorraine Smith, of Fort Pierce, Fla. Also familiar with that phrase is Bruce Carlson, of Cincinnati, who jumped right off the deep end in pursuit of the goal, writing: "I suggest a combination of two phrases my parents used to use: my mother's 'Well, I guess you missed the boat on that one, Bruce,' and my father's comment while reading the evening paper, 'Those bastards are really on the gravy train, aren't they?' My suggestion for a phrase describing arriving after a heyday, therefore, would be *missing the gravy boat*."

But here's an existing twist that's apt, out of the ordinary, and succinct: "The deaf have a sign for the word: *train-go-sorry*," wrote Kathleen Rudden, of Brooklyn, N.Y.

U

"Often after I've heard of something for the first time—a food, a place, a person—I start hearing about it everywhere. Shouldn't there be a word for this?"

—Mark Pener, Somerville, Mass.

"In line with the current trend toward pathologizing every possible mental state," Peter Buchwald, of Akron, Ohio, suggested, "this should be called *attention-surplus disorder*." Then again, maybe it should be called *newbiquitous* (Royce Alden, of Coquille, Ore.). "I hate to borrow from French," Rich Pasenow, of Sacramento, Calif., wrote, "but how about *déjà new*?" Appropriately enough, soon after Pasenow submitted this idea, a version of the phrase turned up elsewhere—in the title, *Déjà Nu*, of a new album by the pop-music star Dion.

This very question, as has been mentioned, exemplifies déjà newness. It appeared on *The Atlantic*'s Web site in January of 1999, and I chose it again for the debut Word Fugitives column that was published in the magazine itself, in February of 2001—it would be pleasingly metaphysical to have this question pop up someplace new, I thought. The cosmic joke was on me: the question turns out to be one that people keep asking and asking. Still, none of the various coinages has caught on. Even now I get mail asking for a word to be coined to meet this need.

U

"What's a word for a situation in which you refuse to accept that the occurrence of two events is merely coincidental but there is no evidence to link them together?"
—*Michael J. Connelly, New York City*

Clever neologisms are certainly possible (aren't they always?). For instance, *fauxincidence*, *coincivince*, *coincidon't*, *duperstition*, and *wishful linking*. But in this case an especially large number of people are convinced that the word sought already exists. Clement J. Colucci, of the Bronx, N.Y., wrote, "The word *apophenia* was coined for that condition in 1958." *The Skeptic's Dictionary*, by Robert Todd Carroll, bears Colucci out ("Apophenia is the spontaneous perception of connections and meaningfulness of unrelated phenomena"). Standard dictionaries, however, do not list the word.

Tom Johnson, of Morris, Minn., reported, "The term *illusory correlation* has been used for many years in the behavioral sciences." And Jan Swearingen, of Bryan, Texas, wrote: "In more than one religious tradition the discipline of *discernment* is taught and encouraged through reflection, meditation, or prayer. *Discernment* is the ability to sense the deeper meaning of similarities, repetitions, and echoes among otherwise random and 'coincidental' events."

Many people proposed **synchronicity**, explaining that this meaning for the word originated with the psychologist Carl Jung. Robert Barth, of Salt Lake City, supplied a definitive reference. He wrote: "In his book *Synchronicity: An Acausal Connecting Principle*, published in 1952, Carl Gustav Jung coined the word to describe such events and advanced the following definition: 'Synchronicity . . . consists of two factors: *(a)* An unconscious image comes into consciousness either directly (i.e., literally) or indirectly (symbolized or suggested) in the form of a dream, idea, or premonition. *(b)* An objective situation coincides with this content. The one is as puzzling as the other.'" How true!

U

"I wonder if there is a word for what happens when teachers, like me, grade papers at the end of terms: the incorrect information in students' papers makes me begin to question my own knowledge. For instance, after grading quite a few papers I begin to ask myself if it is *effect* or *affect*; does Switzerland really border a sea? Is there a word to describe this acute sense of 'unlearning'?"

—*Sriram Khe, Eugene, Ore.*

Temporary inanity is what college English teacher Laura Zlogar, of River Falls, Wis., calls the malady. Deborah Carter, of Walkersville, Md., wrote, "I'm a teacher too, and I've always thought of this phenomenon as *wisdumb*."

Various people suggested *factigue*, *examnesia*, and *misleducation*—also *amissgivings* (Anutosh Moitra, of Sammamish, Wash.), *bogmindling* (Eunice Van Loon, of Biloxi, Miss.), *contaminotion* (Jim Lemon, of Gladesville, of New South Wales, Australia), *errattled* (Lisa Bergtraum, of New York City), *nonsensery overload* (C. Bernard Barfoot, of Alexandria, Va.), *numbleminded* (Doug and Kay Overbey, of Maryville, Tenn.), and *righter's block* (Carol DeMoranville, of Steward, Ill.).

Tom Dorman, of Sedro-Woolley, Wash., had yet another

idea, and he knows whereof he speaks. He wrote: "As a high school teacher, I can sympathize. My ninth-graders have recently convinced me that the Norman Conquest took place in 1951, that Samson and Goliath had a torrid affair (don't tell the school board), and that *car pedium* means 'seize your movement.' Correct tests like this late into the night to meet your grade deadline and you, too, will feel ***doubt-witted*** by your students."

U

"Is there a word for the common experience of saying something to your child and then realizing—often with a shock— that you sound like one of your own parents?"

—Paul von Hippel, Columbus, Ohio

It turns out that an awful lot of people who start to answer this question forget that the word sought is for the realization, rather than for sounding like one's parent.

Some ideas of this latter kind are gender-specific: Beth A. Norris, of Olathe, Kan., wrote, "After having my first child, I quickly realized I had experienced a *mamamorphosis*—I had turned into my mother." Elizabeth Norton, of Columbus, Ohio, suggested the subtle *mnemomic*. A father-related coinage submitted by many people was *patterfamilias*; Graham Arnold, of Harbor City, Calif., suggested *vox pop*.

Other possibilities are *nagatavism* (Jean-Phillipe Wispelaere, of Beaumont, Texas), *parentriloquism* (Mike Reiss, of Los Angeles), and *onomatoparentia* (Elliot Kriegsman, of New York City).

But what about a word for the realization? Maybe *parentnoia* or a variation on that theme? Also possible are twists on *déjà vu* (not again!)—such as *déjà vous* (Kevin McGee, of Oshkosh, Wis.) and *theyja you* (Matt Haugh, of Salem, Ore.). And here's a choice one: ***déjà vieux*** (Randy Miller, of Washington, D.C.). Anyone who is experiencing *déjà new* right now gets extra-credit points for paying close attention.

U

"My husband and I are in search of a word for the fear of throwing a party and having no one show up."
—*Susan Cockrell, Holden, Maine*

What about *guestlessness* or *empty-fest syndrome* (both proposed by many people), *qualmaraderie* (Dawn M. Reeler, of Atlanta), or *fiestanoguestaphobia* (Zach Wechsler, of Los Angeles)? Drew Slatton, of Mount Tabor, N.J., wrote: "This annoying little fear, which manifests itself as a hole in the pit of one's stomach, is known as *guestnoenteritis*." Judy Wagner, of Philadelphia, wrote: "As a former event planner, I can identify. *Humilibration* pretty much sums it up for me."

INNER LIVES GONE BAD

Five of these fifteen words about mental states are diagnoses listed in the American Psychiatric Association's *Diagnostic and Statistical Manual of Mental Disorders*, fourth edition. Five other words appear in the *Oxford English Dictionary*. And five are idiosyncratic coinages, not given in standard reference works. Which words are which?

Acrasia: the state of mind in which you act against your better judgment

Befrought: to be overwhelmed mentally

Caffeine intoxication: characterized by hyperactivity, nervousness, excitability, and/or heart palpitations

Chronovigilitis: compulsive clock-watching

Dissociative fugue: a state of confusion resulting from sudden, unexpected travel

Factitious disorder: faking or intentionally producing physical or psychological symptoms

Formication: a tactile hallucination involving the sensation that things are crawling on or under one's skin

Intermittent explosive disorder: characterized by violent outbursts of rage

Oniomania: a compulsive urge to buy things

Rhytiscopia: an obsession with facial wrinkles

Semiopathy: a tendency to read humorously inappropriate meanings into signs

Shared psychotic disorder: also known as *folie à deux*

Uranomania: the delusion that one is of heavenly descent

Veralgia: the pain associated with seeing things as they truly are

Woofits: an unwell feeling, especially a headache; a moody depression; a hangover

THE DIAGNOSES

Who's got what.

Acrasia is in the *Oxford English Dictionary* (and also in *More Weird and Wonderful Words*).

Befrought was coined by Lewis Burke Frumkes and appears in his "A Volley of Words."

Caffeine intoxication is listed in *DSM-IV* as a psychiatric disorder. The *OED* does not include the term but defines *caffeism* as a similar "morbid condition."

Chronovigilitis is the invention of Roland Drake, of Donaldston, Prince Edward Island, according to *More Brave New Words*.

Dissociative fugue is listed in *DSM-IV* as a psychiatric disorder.

Factitious disorder is listed in *DSM-IV*.

Formication is in the *OED* (and in *The Disheveled Dictionary*).

Intermittent explosive disorder is listed in *DSM-IV*.

Oniomania is in the *OED*.

Rhytiscopia appears in *There's a Word for It*. Psychiatrists would call this obsession a *body dysmorphic disorder*.

Semiopathy, according to *Weird and Wonderful Words*, seems to have been coined by the editors of the Feedback section of *New Scientist* magazine.

Shared psychotic disorder is listed in *DSM-IV*.

Uranomania appears in the *OED* (and in *There's a Word for It*).

Veralgia was coined by the writer Lawrence Shames and appears in *In a Word*.

Woofits is in the *OED* (and in *Weird and Wonderful Words*).

But someone else who can identify sees it differently—more positively, thank goodness. The word that Kathleen DeBold, of Burtonsville, Md., came up with suggests a slight shift of mindset to make party-givers' anticipation less stressful. DeBold wrote: "I am the executive director of a small nonprofit, and we rely on fundraising events for a third of our income. I know too well the dreaded feeling that our party will be a bomb. I call it *fête-alism*."

U

"There are more than a hundred phobias listed in specialized dictionaries. But is there a word for the fear of inadvertently throwing something valuable out with the garbage? Two years ago I found my ring with precious stones in the garbage just before I was about to put it out on the driveway. Since then I always check the garbage bags twice before putting out the trash. I am sure at least a few other people have this fear."
—*Manish Patwari, Montreal, Quebec*

Zillions of *phobia* coinages are possible here. Evidently some of the people inspired to invent them suffer from neither *doxophobia* (fear of expressing opinions) nor *neophobia* (fear of anything new or novel) nor even *catagelophobia* (fear of being ridiculed). Jacob de Jager, of Bountiful, Utah, proposed *discardphobia*; Yvonne R. Freund, of Portland, Ore., the hard-to-pronounce *dumphobia*;

Elizabeth B. Chast, of Brooklyn, the Francophilic *jeteraphobia*; and Walter F. Tanski, of Troy, N.Y., the Hellenologophobic (that is, evidencing a fear of Greek terms) *throwawayoopsaphobia*. Ivan Cooper, of Traverse City, Mich., offered up a nice variation on the theme: *phthrobia*.

The apparently Hellenologophilic Crawford MacKeand, of Greenville, Del., suggested "the too-little-known word **losthrophobia**." He went on to explain: "That current editions of the standard reference works appear to have passed it over is unfortunate, as it brings with it an interesting history. Although folk etymology embraces an obvious derivation, it is of course to the classical Greek, and especially that of Homer, that we should turn for a full understanding. While Liddell & Scott's *Greek-English Lexicon* offers us the Attic, it is clearly to the Homeric that we should turn (*A Lexicon of the Homeric Dialect*, Cunliffe R. J., Blackie, London 1924). This had the well-established significance of 'most agreeable' or 'most advisable,' presumably identical to the unattested Koine word. The sense-inversion phenomenon in the English word is worthy of note, though not uncommon in derivative terminology, e.g., *longshanks* for a notably short person. A connection with loss, and with inadvertent discard, appears to have arisen at a relatively recent date, possibly even in our own century."

Never mind that according to a highly diplomatic e-mail from Samantha Schad, Ph.D., the senior assistant editor responsible for the classical component of etymologies in the *Oxford English Dic-*

tionary, MacKeand's account amounts to a gossamer of information laid delicately upon utter nonsense. That's the name of the game around here. ***Losthrophobia*** it is.

U

"Being able to name my problem may be half the battle. Is there a word for a fear of running over squirrels?"
—Jeff M. Sellers, Glen Ellyn, Ill.

Oh, good—more phobias. For instance, Larry Neckar, of Blue River, Wis., wrote: "I'm a rural mail carrier in a heavily wooded area and am no stranger to various critters (woodchucks, raccoons, squirrels, skunks, and rabbits) acting out their death wishes beneath the wheels of my car. I would call the fear of experiencing the thud, crunch, and sight of the writhing animal in my rearview mirror *flattenfaunaphobia*."

"I personally detest squirrels, as they have the vile habit of digging up my tiny garden," wrote Mike O'Neil, of Sunnyvale, Calif. He, among others, thinks the word should be *roadentaphobia* or *roadentphobia*. Another, more elaborate option is *dentarodentaphobia* (Robert Pollock, of Roseburg, Ore).

Judith Ghoneim, of Charlotte, N.C., suggested the Latinate *sciuruscideaphobia*. It's true that the word *squirrel* came to us by way of Latin, but, as other correspondents kept in mind, it didn't orig-

PHOBIAPHILIA!

❦·❦

Here are some phobias together with my sources for them. I've listed exactly a dozen in order to avoid frightening the triskaidekaphobic—people who are afraid of the number thirteen. (Yes, I know: triskaidekaphobia makes thirteen.)

Ergophobia is a fear of work. According to the Web site World Wide Words, "The word was coined by a doctor named W. D. Spanton, writing in the *British Medical Journal* in 1905."

Friendorphobia is a fear of forgetting a password (as in "Who goes there?"). According to Paul Dickson in his book *Words*, it was coined by a reader of J. Baxter Newgate's National Challenge, a humor column of a few decades ago.

Iraqnophobia is a fear of Iraq or Iraqis. According to *Word Spy*, it began appearing in the media when Iraq invaded Kuwait, in 1990. *Word Spy* notes that "the movie *Arachnophobia* was playing in theaters at the time."

Mysophobia is "a fear of healthy soup, no, a fear of dirt or defilement," according to *Xenia.*

Opecaphobia is a "fear of the price of gasoline going up while it's being pumped into your car." It was coined by John Ficarra in the March 1981 issue of *Mad* magazine.

Orthopolitiphobia is a fear of political correctness. According to private correspondence from the professional wordsmith Charles Harrington Elster, this is a coinage of his.

Psychophobia is either a fear of being attacked in the shower or fear of the mind, according to *There's a Word for It*. According to *Sniglets*, it's "the compulsion, when using a host's bathroom, to peer behind the shower curtain and make sure no one is waiting for you."

Seen-o-phobia is the compulsion to close the door when using the bathroom, even when no one else is home. It was coined by Vivian Lichtenstein, of Rockville, Md., as reported in Bob Levey's column in *The Washington Post*.

Spectocloacophobia is a fear of one's eyeglasses falling into the hole in a Porta-Potti. It was coined by the journalist L. J. Davis, for *In a Word*.

Spritzophobia is a fear of getting caught in the rain without an umbrella. It appears in *Not the Webster's Dictionary*.

Thermalophobia is a fear when showering that someone will sneak in, flush the toilet, and scald you to death. It appears in *Sniglets*.

Typophobia is a fear of finding typographical errors. It was coined by the language maven Richard Dowis, according to *There's a Word for It*.

→·←

inate there. Alex Mattera, of Gloucester, Mass., wrote, "*Squirrel* comes from the combination of the Greek words for 'shadow' and 'tail' "—and just for the heck of it he penned an acrostic poem in honor of squirrels. It begins "Shadow and tail, together the name, / Quiet as nightfall, quick as a flame." Thanks, Alex!

Two people submitted terms they considered to be properly formed from the Greek. Thomas B. Lemann, of New Orleans, sent in *cataballoskiourophobia*, accompanied by supporting photocopies of the pages from a Greek/English dictionary containing "squirrel" and "run over, knock down." Lena Patsidou, of Houston, submitted *skiouroktonophobia*, though she added: "The only places you would see squirrels in Greece are American movies and zoos!" When I consulted Samantha Schad, Ph.D., of the *Oxford English Dictionary*, about these two coinages, she warned, "Obviously it is difficult to have a native speaker's feel for these things." But she went on to say that *skiouroktonophobia* seems likelier to fit the patterns of word formation "that one might expect in Greek."

Then again, why does this fear have to be called a phobia? Why do we need Latin or Greek or pseudo-either? *Squerrulousness* (Beth Kressel, of Highland Park, N.J.) is pretty good. So is *squittishness* (John Ramos, of Duluth, Minn.). We're getting there! At last, here's a right-on-target coinage: ***swervousness*** (John Strasius, of Chicago).

RUSTLED UP

The writer and radio and television personality Roy Blount Jr. was one of the people I asked if they had any neologisms they'd be willing to share. To judge by his response, Blount's inner life is exceptionally unruly. He wrote me:

My daughter Ennis, when she was a little girl, once spoke of a *rumpity ride*, meaning roughly "merrily bouncy," I would say, but when I pressed her (sounding perhaps overfascinated) for a definition, she changed the subject. She may have pulled back, at that moment, from a career in bardism. *Bardry? Barding?*

Because *accomplice*, to me, connotes subordination—an accessory or a henchman—I have occasionally felt I needed the word *complicitor*. But I've been persuaded by dictionaries, every time, that my sense of *accomplice* rests upon misinference. (There, is that one?) And whereas a solicitor solicits, there is no such verb as *complicit*. "According to his testimony, he did not know of the plot until he found himself *complicited* in it"? Oh, but wait, you ought to be able to say "He was unaware of the plot until he became one of the *complicitors*." Though I guess "until he became *complicit* in it" is better. But awkward—"licitinit"—to pronounce. Maybe there should be a word like *licitinity* for linguinfelicity caused by too many short "i"s—except that when you turn it into *licitinity* it bounces right along.

My late mother would use the verb *to gibble*, always with *up*, as in "Oh, you've *gibbled up* that styrofoam all over the floor," or "Our best snack when I was a girl was to *gibble up* some cornbread in a glass of cold buttermilk." A back-formation from *giblets*, which were cut up in giblet gravy. I think it's a good, useful word. She would also say to a small child whose ears she was trying to wash, "Don't *squirmle* so much."

I think the term *postmature*, as regards a stage in life or something put off too long, has (so to speak) possibilities. Is there a word for that *so to speak*, whereby a writer attempts to point out—to make sure the reader notices that the writer is aware of—certain or rather uncertain sort-of-notable, we might say *infrapunny* (oh Jesus) verbal reverberations that have cropped up . . . Never mind.

> *Schnicker*: a drunken snicker
> *Scraction*: tires getting going on a loose surface
> *Scrimptious*: as opposed to *scrumptious*
> *Scrotch*: scratch/crotch

The portmanteau word *chortle* is good. My hat is off to *chortle*. You can't force new words, counterfeit coinage.

Wendalyn Nichols, a lexicographer and the editor of *Copy Editor* newsletter, wrote me:

My best friend throughout my school years was someone who could nearly always be relied upon to get a word wrong. Sometimes, though, her creations were far more apt than the word she was seeking. One that stuck was *distrewed*. I still don't quite know how to spell it. She was describing the way she'd reacted when a boy she liked suddenly asked her out, and she said, "Oh, I got all *distrewed*." I think she was searching for *distraught*, blended it with *confused*—and voilà. We used *distrewed* for years.

And Bill Walsh, the national-desk copy chief of *The Washington Post*, has one more word to add to our inner-life lexicon. He wrote me:

My wife, Jacqueline Dupree, uses the adjective *blork* to refer to a feeling of fullness bordering on sickness.

"Would you like another piece of cheesecake?"

"Are you kidding? I am just *blork*."

It can also be an exclamation. We finish our soufflés at Morton's, we look at each other, and simultaneously we say, "*Blork!*"

STILL AT LARGE

Finally, here are some fugitives about our ever-unruly inner lives for which your help is sought:

"I would like a word for the opposite of *déjà vu*[!]—a word that would describe the feeling of learning something a hundred times but never being able to remember it."

—*Andrew Felcher, Portland, Ore.*

"At unpredictable intervals my wife gets a sudden powerful urge to move things around—pictures, furniture, potted plants, whatever. What can we call that urge?"

—*Bernard Weissman, Los Angeles*

"I'd like a coinage for the mistaken assumption that an out-of-the-limelight celebrity is deceased."

—*Scott Mehno, New York City*

"In my travels, I've often wanted a name to express the fear of leaving something in a hotel room. I find myself checking behind furniture and in drawers I didn't use."

—*Mike Sigler, Nashville, Tenn.*

"What would be a word for wanting to get someone's voice mail but getting the person instead?"

—*Cullen Murphy, Medfield, Mass.*

"What do you call a catchy melody or jingle that keeps replaying in your head and you can't stop it?"

—*Glenn Davis, Mountain View, Calif.*

"How about a word for the dreams we can't remember, the ones that are lost?"

—*John A. Knowles, Walnut Creek, Calif.*

"I'd like a name for the feeling you get when an arrogant person raises an objection or contradicts you too quickly."

—*Rosamond Purcell, Medford, Mass.*

"How about a word for the anxiety resulting from food spilled on pale clothing at the beginning of an evening out?"

—*Rosemary Holland and Ian Huckabee,*
Southern Pines, N.C.

"Please give me a word for a mental state that results from parking in the same garage or lot every day: the temporary confusion I experience when I head back to the car after work and wonder where I parked it this time."

—*Julian H. Fisher, Brookline, Mass.*

"I have a phobia about marching units in parades. Whenever I see a band or military unit marching in formation toward me, I burst into tears. I've had this problem for many years, perhaps dating back to the televised funeral for President Kennedy. Otherwise, I'm perfectly normal! What is the word for my phobia?"

—*Ann Milam, Seattle*

2

THEM

W hy is it that there never seem to be enough words in the dictionary to cover everyone we dislike? To make things worse, new kinds of dislikable people keep cropping up.

Shall we look on the sunny side for a sec? A number of old reasons to disparage people are passé. Insulting terms for members of particular ethnicities, gays, blondes, women in general, old people, the disabled, etc., are *so* early twentieth century. Not only that, but our society has managed to break cycles of abuse of much longer standing. Epithets like *lackey*, *churl*, and *mountebank*; *poltroon*, *pander*, and *strumpet*; *coxcomb*, *popinjay*, and *varlet* are scarcely ever hurled anymore.

To look on the snarky side, that's not all to the good—or at least, the part about the epithets is not. Those ringing words all belonged to Shakespeare's vocabulary. Lackeys ("servile followers; toadies") and churls ("rude and boorish" or "miserly" people) and all the rest of those kinds of dislikable people still plague us. We just hurl different, cruder epithets at them.

Bring back the old, I say! But let's also bring on the new. Why? Because today there are more kinds of dingalings in heaven and earth than were dreamt of in Shakespeare's philosophy.

U

"I'd love to have a term for those people who leave long, rambling messages on answering machines and then rattle off their phone numbers at lightning speed in the last second, forcing you to repeat the entire message to get the all-important digits."

—Marc Burckhardt, Austin, Texas

Of all the people who responded to this request, exactly two dared to admit that they'd ever left such messages themselves. Steve Billington, of Vancouver, British Columbia, confessed, "Sadly, I am among the guilty," and suggested the coinage "*idiodidactiphone*: a foolish information provider on your telephone." Eric C. Besch, of Fayetteville, N.C., began his response by explaining himself:

"Somehow I am always befuddled not to have a person answer my call." Besch suggested the adjective *prolixety-split*.

Ted Garon, of Mission Viejo, Calif., wrote not to propose a word but to share his solution to the problem, which, he boasted, has "failed only once in the past three years." His answering-machine message is carefully enunciated and ends like this: "Please say your phone number slowly. We have an elderly butler."

David P. Nagle, a college professor in Norman, Okla., had no sympathy whatsoever for the perpetrators who get in touch with him: "students whose breathless cell-phone messages fall into cell hell right after a 'dog ate my homework' statement, during the 'please call me right away at [unintelligible]' finale." Nagle's coinage was a variant on what was probably the most popular suggestion: *prestodigitators*.

And Gregory Pierce, of New York City, wrote: "As an English tutor, I've had to listen to epic phone messages from high schoolers who are in the 'diction is uncool' phase. After listening to a long chain of *um*s and *uh*s, I usually can't understand the crucial digits at the end. I call these people *number-mumblers*. Since there have been so many, I've recently shortened the term to ***numblers***." Neat!

U

"Is there a word to describe someone who can read but can't pronounce words? One such person I know, who learned English from books, says things like 'Follow the gweed at the cathedral.'"

—*Jean P. Bell, Ontario, N.Y.*

Jake Fey, of Berlin, Germany, wrote: "As an English teacher abroad, I often run into this phenomenon. These students may learn to read English, but they definitely do not speak English. Instead, I tell them, they speak *Booklish*."

Carol Takyi, of Sherwood Park, Alberta, wrote that her husband, "as a young West African arriving to study in the United States in the fifties, learned to pronounce many English words the hard way—for instance, by going to a music store and asking to look at their *hee-fees*." And Patrick McDougall, of Montreal, Quebec, wants it on record that he had a thirty-seven-year career as a radio announcer despite having pronounced, in his early days on the job, "*misled* to rhyme with *whistled* and *infrared* to rhyme with *compared*." Surely we've all fallen victim at one time or another—for instance, when faced with *Goethe* or *Hippocrates*, *Thucydides* or *Liberace*, *chimera* or *paradigm*. But what to call the condition? More than one person suggested the nifty coinage *tome-deaf*; he who proposed it first was Don Slutes, of Phoenix.

P.S.: Did you have any trouble decoding *gweed*? It's standing in for *guide*, of course.

U

"I'm sitting in my cubicle wondering why there isn't a word for people who send e-mail messages and then follow them up saying, 'Did you get my e-mail message?' It would certainly be nice to have a label for them."

—*Tom Okawara, Evanston, Ill.*

This is a surprisingly divisive question. "I take issue with the blatant attack on those of us who send follow-up e-mails," wrote Andrew Goldberg, of New York City. Cheryl Scott Ryan, of Austin, Texas, wrote, "Our recent office move has not been kind to our outgoing e-mail, so I feel a need to make sure all my e-mails make it to their intended recipients." Ryan, among many others, proposed the bias-free term *re-mailers* to describe people like her.

Suzanne Lanoue, of Tuscaloosa, Ala., advised, "They may be doing it for a good reason, such as that it is an important matter to them and you didn't answer them in good time." She continued: "How about a word for people who never read their e-mail? Or a word for people who never answer it? And what about for those self-centered people who reply to your e-mail but don't answer any of your questions or don't make comments about anything you said?"

Most people, however, heaped scorn on e-mailers who follow up, suggesting such unflattering terms as *cybores* (coined by Marjory Wunsch, of Cambridge, Mass.), *confirmaniacs* (Sheridan Manasen, of Kennebunk, Maine), *memorons* (Phil Ruder, of Forest Grove, Ore.), and *e-diots* (proposed by several people). Mitchell Burnside Clapp, of Los Olivos, Calif., wrote: "I suggest *NetWit*, with the irregular capitalization appropriate to the computer age. I think a hideous neologism is needed to describe the hideous reality."

John G. Keresty, of Vernon, N.J., shared an observation about a similar behavior in a different realm. He wrote: "Years ago I was in the sportswriting business, and I found that every coach of any sport at any level would repeat short instructions or exhortations thus: 'Let's go get 'em, let's go get 'em'; 'Good job, Keresty, good job'; 'Hey, ref, hey, ref! Are you blind? Are you blind?' and so on, and so on. So for the quest for a word for e-mail follow-uppers, I give you the one I coined for all the double-speak coaches: ***redundunces***." Very nice. Very nice.

P.S.: To everyone who responded electronically to this question in *The Atlantic* and then sent a follow-up e-mail cheekily asking whether I'd received that response, Yes, I did, thanks!

IF THESE ARE ANSWERS, WHAT WAS THE QUESTION?

Here are a few responses to a challenge issued by *The Washington Post*'s Style Invitational contest. To come up with these words, what were readers asked to do?

Diddleman: a person who adds nothing but time to an effort (Mark Bowers, Alexandria, Va.)

Errorist: a member of a radical Islamic cult who blows himself up in a mannequin factory (Barry Blyveis, Columbia, Md.)

The fundead: corpses who walk around at night with lampshades on their heads (Jonathan Paul, Garrett Park, Md.)

Nominatrix: a spike-heeled woman who controls the selection of candidates for party whip (Chris Doyle, Forsyth, Mo.)

Philaunderer: a man who hops from bed to bed but always washes the sheets (Malcolm Fleschner, San Mateo, Calif.)

Tskmaster: an ineffective slave driver (Jonathan Paul, Garrett Park, Md.)

Urinpal: a guy who uses the one right next to you even though all the others are unoccupied (Dominic Casario, Tampa, Fla.)

Whorde: a group of prostitutes (Bird Waring, New York City)

The Style Invitational challenged readers to "take any word, add, subtract, or alter a single letter, and redefine the word."

U

If the answers commonly suggested include *audiots, cellfish, cellots, cellulouts, earheads, earitants, incellferables, imbecells, jabberwonks,* and *phonies,* what is the question? Here goes:

"We all encounter people in cars, airports, and shopping centers who seem to have a cell phone glued to one of their ears. I would like to have a word to describe these people."
                                    —*Mike Lewiecki, Albuquerque, N.M.*

Usually when Word Fugitives reckons with people whose habits are unsavory, at least a few respondents rise to the defense of the people in question. Not this time.

Russ Newsom, of Charlotte, N.C., suggested the word *phoneglommer* but, rather than explaining that, told this tale: "I was involved in a car accident, and one man, the cause, was cut on his forehead. I approached his car and, trying to remember my Red Cross training, said simply, 'Are you OK?' He was in his front seat, bleeding profusely. He continued talking on his phone and held out one forefinger to me—the 'Hold on one second' gesture."

Brian Flanagan, of Boston, came about as close as anyone to expressing solidarity with cell-phone users: "An appropriate word to describe these people, whose chatter we resent and yet whose ranks we are all too ready to join when our own cell phones ring, might be *cell mates*, conveying that we're all pretty efficiently imprisoned in this cellular world."

But, of course, we do resent others' loud public chatter, and the word requested was meant to reflect that. A coinage that does is **yakasses,** from Tim Weiner, of Mexico City.

U

"A friend has a habit of taking a lovely song and changing one or two words to make it vulgar—which he thinks is funny. The next time the song is played, I 'hear' his crude version and not the actual rendition. Many of my favorite songs have been ruined in this manner. What would you call this? And is there a name for him?"

—Deborah Redden, McDonough, Ga.

Who knew that the lyrics to "Amazing Grace" can be sung to the tune of the *Gilligan's Island* theme song? ("Amazing grace! How sweet the sound / That saved a wretch like me! / I once was lost, but now am found; / Was blind, but now I see." "Ta-dum-dum-dah, ta-dee-dee-dee / Ta-dum-dum-dah-dah-dee," etc.) Well, the Reverend Monsignor Richard Soseman, of Princeville, Ill., knew it, and graciously shared the information. The practice for which we are seeking a name is similar to one that from time to time has claimed Soseman's attention—namely, "taking sacred lyrics and singing them to secular tunes." Soseman lamented, "Once heard this way, they never sound the same again."

A number of other people sent in examples of vulgarized lyrics, thereby earning themselves the right to be called by whatever a name would be for people who do this. A few people suggested *bawdlerize* and *bawdlerizer*, and others *scat* and *scat singer*. Lori Corbett, of St. Anthony, Idaho, suggested *misongeny* and *misongenist*. A group identifying itself as "The English Class of the Ministry of the Interior," in Bonn, Germany, wrote: "We would like to suggest *mislieder*. The act, of course, would be *mislieding*."

Not everyone who responded sent in a matched pair of words. Mike McDonald, of San Francisco, played around with *mondegreen*, which the *American Heritage Dictionary* defines as "a series of words that result from the mishearing or misinterpretation of a statement or song lyric," to get *mondeblue* for naughty lyrics. Words suggested for the singer include *songwronger* and *leericist*

THE WAY THEY DO THE THINGS THEY DO

These qualities, abilities, and attributes apply to certain
of *them*. Can you match the coinages with their definitions
or descriptions?

1. The bravura born of owning many trendy
   objects   *Careersma*
2. Congenitally incapable of ever having a
   paper tissue   *Dobermanners*
3. Disagreeable eating habits   *Hankate*
4. Distasteful or ugly   *Hideola*
5. Evilly busy, up to no good   *Malactive*
6. Fully confident, even in the complete
   absence of evidence, that others share their
   high opinions of themselves   *Mimbridge*
7. Indicating a sort of conscious aristocracy . . .
   that resides, but does not live; that becomes
   ill, but is never taken sick; . . . whose life, in
   short, consists in trying to conceal the fact
   that a spade is nothing but an agricultural
   implement   *Muchismo*
8. Intelligent-looking but dim-witted   *Not clueful*
9. "It sounds a lot more positive than *clueless*"   *Obsniptious*
10. Spectacular but essentially bogus facility for
    career advancement   *Ponis*
11. That which two very boring people have in
    common which enables you to get away
    from them   *Pronoid*
12. The thinning ponytail that balding boomers
    wear in a desperate effort to stem the
    ravages of middle-age hair loss   *Superfacial*

THE WAY THEY DO, PART 2

Here's what was coined, and where.

1. **Muchismo** is trendy-object-related bravura. The word was coined by the writer Lia Matera, for *In a Word*.
2. **Hankate** means "never carrying a tissue" in *The Deeper Meaning of Liff*. Otherwise, it is the name of a village in of Overijssel, the Netherlands.
3. **Dobermanners** means "disagreeable eating habits," according to *Not the Webster's Dictionary*.
4. **Hideola** is sometimes said to have been coined by W. H. Auden, and it appears in his poetry. But both Chester Kallman, a librettist and translator and Auden's lover, and their friend Harold Norse, a poet, have laid claim to the word; Auden picked up *hideola* from one of them. Later, Truman Capote did, too, in *Breakfast at Tiffany's*.
5. **Malactive** is defined as "evilly busy" in "A Volley of Words."
6. **Pronoid** is the word for "confident . . . that others share their high opinion of themselves." It was coined by the journalist Avery Rome.
7. **Obsniptious** means "indicating a sort of conscious aristocracy," according to the 1908 article "Improvised Words."
8. **Superfacial** is defined as "intelligent-looking but dim-witted" in *Not the Webster's Dictionary*.
9. **Not clueful** was coined for the reason given by Julia MacLauchlan, while she was general manager of the Natural Language Group at Microsoft. Others have coined it, too, and now *clueful* appears in the *New Oxford American Dictionary*, second edition.
10. **Careersma,** facility for career advancement, was coined by Professor Gerald Graff, for *In a Word*.
11. **Mimbridge** is what two boring people have in common, according to *The Deeper Meaning of Liff*. Elsewhere, according to the English Place-Name Society, it is believed to have been "a bridge by an ancient mint once recorded" in the area of Chobham, southwest of London.
12. **Ponis,** for a thinning ponytail on a balding boomer, was coined by Patrick Kincaid, of Delta, British Columbia, in *Wanted Words*.

(each proposed by a number of people), *ribaldefiler* (Romy Benton, of Portland, Ore.), *opporntunist* (Steve Groulx, of Cornwall, Ontario), *verse-vicer* (Nancy Schimmel, of Berkeley, Calif.), and the cute *humdinger* (Diana K. Colvin, of Portland, Ore.)—a word that might work equally well for the song.

Peter Grant, of St. Catherines, Ontario, was the first of a few people to send in ***perversifier*** or ***perversification***—very nice, no? Let's all sing Grant a rousing chorus of "Four-Cheese Tamales and Jell-O."

U

"As you know, the word *hysteria* has its origins in female physiology, and it applies to the manner in which women behave when stressed. The word was probably coined by men, who, I'm sure, found this behavior of women incomprehensible. It has always seemed to me that there should be a word for the way men behave when stressed. I have on a number of occasions found myself strapped in the passenger seat of a car flying down the highway at top speed while the male driver of my car was chasing another driver and screaming, 'You SOB!' I am as mystified about this male behavior as men must be about hysterical female behavior."

—*Marcia Pollack, Kingston, N.J.*

MAIM THAT TUNE

❖·❖

The term *mondegreen*, meaning "misheard song lyrics," was coined by the writer Sylvia Wright in a 1954 article in *Harper's*. As she reported there, when she was a child she heard the seventeenth-century Scottish ballad "The Bonny Earl of Murray," whose first stanza goes like this: "Ye Highlands and ye Lawlands, / O where hae ye been? / They hae slain the Earl of Murray, / And hae laid him on the green." To her, that last line sounded like "And Lady Mondegreen"—hence her coinage. These days *mondegreen* is also used for lyrics that have been intentionally, irreverently revised.

Some cases in point:

From traditional songs and hymns
> Here comes the bride / All fat and wide.
> I want a girl just like the girl that harried dear old Dad.
> Jimmy crapped corn and I don't care.
> Tie a yellow ribbon 'round the old roast beef.
> Don't cry for me, Marge and Tina.
> Stand beside her and guide her / With the light from the bite of a bug.
> I love spareribs in the springtime, I love spareribs in the fall.
> Bradley, the cross-eyed bear.

My eyes have seen the glory of the coming of the
Lord / He has trampled on the village where the
great giraffe is stored.
Onward Christian Soldiers, marching out the door!

From Beatles songs
And when I get home to you, I find a broken canoe.
She was a gay stripper.
I'll never dance with your mother since your fa-
ther's standing there.
She's got a chicken to fry, / and she don't care.
Lovely Rita needs a maid.
Lucy's in a fight with Linus!
If she's beside me / I know I need Medicare.
Let me pee.

Sources: Jon Carroll, in the *San Francisco Chronicle*, and his readers Paul
Baker, of San Bruno, Calif.; Cathy Cox; Ramdass Khalsa, of El Cerrito, Calif.;
and "Susan Smith's mother"; *Atlantic Monthly* readers Andrew G. Ahern III,
of Landenberg, Pa., and Leonard Schoppa, of Charlottesville, Va.; and
www.amiright.com, a Web site overseen by Charles R. Grosvenor Jr.

If each suggestion that came in to Word Fugitives had counted as a vote, the winner by far would have been *testeria*. A number of *histerias*, *hersterias*, and *malestroms* arrived as well. Other possibilities submitted include *malefeasance* (Nancy Strauss, of Excelsior, Minn.), *manic expressive* (Mort Somer, of Ogden, Utah), and *male-pattern badness* (more than one person).

Many people, though, protested that English already contains the necessary term. Some wanted to turn *malevolence* or *mania* to the purpose at hand (among them Tom Doyle, of Bristol, Conn., who pointed out that when used in this sense, *mania* should have the plural form *menia*). A few, including Sam Abrams, of Rochester, N.Y., made a case for *musth*. According to the *Oxford English Dictionary*, Abrams wrote, *musth* is "applied to male animals . . . in a state of dangerous frenzy to which they are subject at irregular intervals." Several people mentioned that *testosterone poisoning* is current in approximately the sense wanted, and yet others suggested that *testiness* might fit the bill.

Maybe a different existing word, though, fits it better. As it happens, the person who thought of this word first also sent it along in a particularly charming letter. Lavaine Peterson, of Cloquet, Minn., proposed **ballistic**, explaining: "Yes, even though I'm almost seventy-two and a devoted Lutheran churchgoer, I am thinking in a somewhat naughty manner. However, if it will do something to cut down on road rage, the embarrassment will be worth it."

RUSTLED UP

I asked the writer, editor, and publisher André Bernard about *them*, and he turned out to have a particular variety on his mind. He wrote me:

Budgers. These are drivers who, instead of politely getting in line behind the other cars at an exit or when lanes are blocked off for road construction, continue driving in the fast lane until the last possible minute and then veer over and budge into the exit in front of other cars, thus slowing down traffic considerably. My wife, Jennie, uses this word constantly—she claims to have coined it. Although I hear her occasionally using it about people who don't observe lines at movie theaters, at the reception desk in restaurants, and in the subway, it seems especially apt on the road. *"Budger!"* she shouts as she maneuvers to force said pushy drivers aside. "It's a *budger!*"

The graphic designer Amy Swan wrote me:

Potato eaters. My husband, Marty Hergert, coined this. We use it to describe the general population when it's massed in an annoying way. An example would be the slow, meandering cart-pushers blocking the aisles and stopping every few feet to read product labels while grocery shopping on Saturday afternoon. The term comes from Van Gogh's painting titled *The Potato Eaters*, which depicts peasants going about their daily dull routines. Van Gogh spoke of the peasants as leading "a way of life completely different from ours, from that of civilized people."

And Dany Levy, the founder and editor of DailyCandy.com, who compiles lexicons of "chick-speak" for her Web site and *Allure* magazine, had a few suggestions:

Helicopter: a significant other who finds it necessary to hover around his or her mate at all times.

Showflake: a person who chronically misses every appointment (e.g., haircuts, doctor visits, dinners).

SoDeeWah: socialite/designer/whatever. The model/actress/whatever of the '00s.

Trophy waif: a trophy wife who is too skinny. Today's answer to *Bonfire of the Vanities's "social X-ray."*

STILL AT LARGE

 Although they themselves may not be sought after, names for them are. Some of them who remain unidentified are . . .

"We have all met procrastinators and understand the term that describes them. But what about the opposite: someone who completes a task as soon as it is assigned? *Obsessive* doesn't quite cover it."

—*Amy Stoutenger, Yorktown, Va.*

"How do you call the man who will soon become your ex-husband? It is the reverse equivalent of *fiancé*. Can you suggest a word that is polite and neutral?"

—*Eden Forsythe*

"I have a desperate need for a word that conveys the essential meaning of the phrase *trailer trash* without maligning innocent dwellings."

—*Karen Cox, Austin, Texas*

"We need a word to describe a person who, owing to his life circumstances, clearly is not competent to provide advice but insists on doing so anyway. For example, an unemployed person who gives advice to a person considering competing professional offers, or a receptionist who unabashedly offers medical advice to a roomful of doctors."

—*Mark Kennet, Kibbutz Manara, Israel*

THE MATERIAL WORLD

A sizable majority of the words that are added to our dictionaries nowadays are names for things. People just won't stop inventing things, and perceiving old things in new ways. And things need names: *blogs*, *infinity pools*, *conflict diamonds*. A separate issue is commercial products, with their expensively, extensively negotiated and marketed names. Standard dictionaries exclude most product and brand names, but the proportion of "new" words that name things rises even higher if you count pre-existing words and phrases that have been turned into brands: *Tiger* (computer operating system), *Magic Hat* (beer), *Juicy Couture* (sportswear), *BlackBerry* (portable communication device).

And yet fugitives—especially captured ones—that name things are relatively rare. I don't know why. Granted, the creators

73

of word fugitives are self-selected. Are we especially otherworldly and nonmaterialistic? Search me. Or maybe the explanation is that things already have names. Consider *aglets* (the tiny plastic wrappers at the ends of shoelaces) and *altocumulus undulatus* (the clouds in a herringbone sky) and *chads* (*you* remember: the little spots of paper that fall off punch cards). There is scarcely a thing so small or ethereal or insignificant or transient that someone somewhere has not named it.

A few of those hitherto-unnamed rarities are on display here. These are followed by fugitives that have to do with our behavior in relation to things, and then by ones having to do with things' behavior in relation to us. The chapter also contains a lexicon of my favorite names for things that have been coined elsewhere.

"How about a word for an object that works only if one employs a trick known to its owner or frequent user, like jiggling it, putting pressure on it, warming it, or blowing on it?"
—*Evelin Sullivan, Redwood City, Calif.*

Some people think of eponyms—in particular, the likes of *fonzie*, *fonzable*, and *fonzer*, all intended to evoke "the Fonz," Henry Winkler's character in the sitcom *Happy Days*, because of his ability to get the jukebox to work by giving it a whack.

Evelin Sullivan, who asked for help in finding this word fugitive in the first place, wrote again to propose a coinage: *jigglit*. A couple of people suggested *fussgadget*. Bob Israel, of Westford, Mass., proposed *computer*, explaining, "I've never seen one that didn't require regular trickery to keep it going." Several people proposed *wife*, *husband*, or *spouse*.

Neologisms beginning with *thingama-* were popular—for instance, *thingamajiggler* and *thingamabobject*. Ones beginning with *idio-* were more popular still. Michael Mates, an officer at the U.S. Consulate General in Karachi, Pakistan, submitted *idiosynpractical*. Nifty word, but we were looking for a noun. Other people suggested *idiosecretic*, *idiopathetic*, *idiosymatic*, and—hooray, some nouns!—*idiosyncrathing* and *idiosyncontraption*. Arun Shankar, of York, Pa., was thinking along these lines too, but he thought a bit more, well, idiosyncretically than most, to arrive at **idiosynamajig**.

U

"What is the accumulation of stuff that collects under your car, behind the wheels, when driving in slush or snow? These lumps are truly hideous-looking, being composed of frozen snow, sand, salt, and road grime. They fall off in the driveway or parking lot, and sit there looking like some repulsive growth until they melt in the spring."

—Duane Douglass, North Berwick, Maine

Apparently, sooner or later just about everybody in the snowy parts of our continent feels a need for this word. On a "Word Fugitives" Web page, Michael Fischer, of Minneapolis, pointed out that *Sniglets* designated such a thing a *fenderberg*. Dan Bloom wrote: "Some years ago, I think this was a word sought from listeners by the gang at NPR's *All Things Considered*. If memory serves, the favored submission was *snard*." I searched the *ATC* archives but, alas, failed to turn up anything relevant. Elsewhere on the Web, though, I discovered that some people use *snard* as an acronym for "Situation Normal, Another Rotten Day" and that others know Snard as the name of a computer "launcher program."

The book *Wanted Words*, however, contains *snards* (submitted by Charlie Kolompar, of Rexdale, Ontario) defined like this: "the muddy ice clumps that form behind car wheels in the winter." And a posting by "2stroked" on F150 Online, "the web site for owners and enthusiasts of the late model Ford F-150 and other full size Ford truck models" (www.F150online.com), shows that *snard* is used this way in the United States too: "First of all—for all you southerners—a *snard* is a collection of snow, ice, salt, road grime (and if you live in New Jersey—Jimmy Hoffa) that builds up behind the wheel wells of your F-150 (or any other vehicle) when you drive in snow." The Web site Urbandictionary (www .urbandictionary.com), a slang-oriented reference source that is being continually written by its users, has an entry for *snardlump* with the same meaning—minus Jimmy Hoffa. *Family Words* also mentions *snard*, though the subject comes up under the heading of *grice* (a word that "combines the words *grime* and *ice*," as the book's author, Paul Dickson, explains).

Michael Christian, of Michigan, sent Word Fugitives **carna-cle**—nice. *Carnacle*, like *snards*, appears in *Wanted Words*, but it's defined as "the coattail, dress hem, or seat belt that hangs out the door of moving vehicles." If dictionary words can have more than one meaning, I suppose there's no reason captured fugitives can't. *Carnacle* works for our purpose too.

U

"The Irish term is *witches' knickers*. But on this side of the Atlantic we don't seem to have a name for disposable plastic bags caught in trees, flapping in the wind."
—*Brendan J. O'Byrne, Regina, Saskatchewan*

This question earned Word Fugitives a scolding from Kathleen Dotoli, of Long Branch, N.J., who wrote, "I do not believe *witches' knickers* should be messed with, as it is a perfect description." Lee Buenaventura, of Wellesley, Mass., felt nearly the same way, but she suggested giving the term a "tweak" to Americanize it: *witches' britches*. Then again, reports of existing American terms arrived from all over. People on both coasts and in between submitted *urban tumbleweed*. R. Matthew Green, of West Kingston, R.I., said that in his state "bags caught in trees, flapping in the wind, are called *shoppers' kites*." Sheilah Zimpel, of Raleigh, N.C., wrote, "Here in the South we call that *white trash*." Samuel Hoffman, of Fort Wayne, Ind., wrote, "Plastic bags trapped in trees and along fence lines are called *bag hawks*."

The query also presented an unexpected opportunity for score-settling among interstate rivals. Kristen Lummis, of Grand Junction, Colo., wrote, "A plastic bag caught in a tree (or a barbed-wire fence), flapping in the wind, is known as *the state bird of Wyoming*." And Richard R. Crowder, of Lynchburg, Va., proposed the term *West Virginia state flag*.

But surely a good descriptor should apply more broadly—even outside the United States, especially since the fellow who requested the word in the first place is Canadian. Suggestions that would be appropriate almost anywhere include *totebirds* (George Campbell, of St. Paul, Minn.), *retailed hawks* (Daniel Scheub, of Dixon, Ill.), *trash kites* (Linda Muhlhausen, of Tinton Falls, N.J.), *treecycled plastic* (Jonathan Stone, of Annapolis, Md.), *Glad® rags* (John R. Ehrenfeld, of Lexington, Mass.), and *detreetus* (Christina Lamb, of Southborough, Mass.).

Daniel Brown, of San Carlos, Calif., wrote, "I suggest *fooliage*, since the bags come from morons careless with their trash." Rob Barendse, of Granville, N.Y., suggested *plastoliage*. Can you see it coming? That's right: ***fouliage***, which was first submitted by Michael Abrams, of Custer, Wash.

ANTIQUES OR NOVELTY ITEMS?

Ten of these are dictionary names (mostly archaic, rare, or dialectal) for things, and ten are family words or recreational coinages. Which are which?

Aquabob: an icicle

Beggars' velvet: downy particles that accumulate under furniture from the negligence of housemaids

Benble: any minor anomaly—sweater pills, for instance

Cinestate: property left by a cineaste

Dunolly: an improvised umbrella

Eaper: any object without an obvious function, such as the kind of thing one is likely to find at the bottom of a box at a rummage sale

Glackett: the noisy ball inside a spray-paint can

Goosecruives: a pair of wooden trousers worn by poultry-keepers in the Middle Ages

A head of thyme: term for the herb in quantity

Hibernacle: a winter retreat, or the winter home of a hibernating animal

Kiddliwink: a small shop where they retail the commodities of a village store

Kikidoori: a pearl-like growth occasionally uncovered during root-canal surgery

Knackatory: a place to buy knickknacks

Nodge: the only one of its kind, or having no mate

Platyplus: a mammal with webbed feet, a duck bill, and opposable thumbs

Quodammodotative: a thing that exists in a certain way

Scatches: stilts worn in the early sixteenth to the nineteenth centuries when walking in filthy places

Tegestology: the collecting of beer mats

Tittynope: a small quantity of anything left over

Zythepsary: a brewhouse

THE OLD SORTED OUT FROM THE NEW

Herewith the dictionary words, their sources, the non-dictionary words, and their coiners.

Aquabob is defined as "an icicle" in *The Word Museum*; its source was an 1838 dictionary of "provincialisms."

Beggars' velvet as a forerunner of *dust bunnies* appears in *The Word Museum* and in the *OED*. Their sources are, respectively, an 1887 slang dictionary and an 1855 dictionary of "archaic and provincial" words.

Benble to mean a "minor anomaly" is a coinage reported to *Family Words* by Cate Pfeifer, of Milwaukee, Wis.

Cinestate, property left by a cineaste, is a neologism appearing in the non-dictionary *Not the Webster's Dictionary*.

Dunolly means "an improvised umbrella" in *The Deeper Meaning of Liff*. Elsewhere it is the name of an Australian town that was once an important gold-mining center.

Eaper, an object without an obvious function, was reported to *Family Words* by a KMOX listener, in St. Louis.

Glackett, the noisy ball inside a spray-paint can, appears in *Sniglets*. *The Deeper Meaning of Liff* gives a similar definition for *Millinocket*, which is otherwise a town in Maine.

Goosecruives are wooden trousers worn by poultry-keepers only in *The Deeper Meaning of Liff*. Elsewhere, *Goosecruives* is the name of a village in Aberdeenshire, Scotland.

A *head* of thyme, referring to the herb in quantity, was coined by Harry Richardson, of Laurel, Md., for The Style Invitational.

Hibernacle, a winter retreat, is given in *More Weird and Wonderful Words* and the *OED*.

Kiddliwink, a small shop, appears in *The Word Museum*. The *OED* also notes this definition, from an 1859 dictionary of slang, where the word is spelled *kiddleliwink*. But *kiddleywink* is the word's primary spelling according to the *OED*, and its primary meaning is "an alehouse, esp. in the West Country; a low or unlicensed public house."

Kikidoori, a pearl-like growth, appears in "A Volley of Words."

Knackatory, a place to buy knickknacks, appears in *More Weird and Wonderful Words* and the *OED*.

Nodge, having no mate, was coined for *Burgess Unabridged*. A few newer near synonyms have to do specifically with socks. Two that are given in *Family Words* are *Robinson Crewsock*, reported by Marlene Aronow, of Deerfield, Ill.; and *lurkin*, "so called because you know the mate is lurkin' around somewhere," according to C. W. Sande, of Caldwell, Idaho.

Platyplus, a name for an impressive imaginary mammal, was coined by Russell Beland, of Springfield, Va., for The Style Invitational.

Quodammodotative appears in the *OED*. *What* does it mean—or, inasmuch as it's obsolete, what did it once mean? Thomas Stanley tried to explain in the 1656 volume of his *History of Philosophy*. He wrote, "Things are subdivided into foure Genus's, Subjects, and Qualitatives and Quodammodotatives in themselves, and Quodammodotatives as to others." Ah, yes. Of course.

Scatches are indeed stilts that were worn when in filthy places, according to *Forgotten English* and the *OED*.

Tegestology, the collecting of beer mats, appears in *Weird and Wonderful Words* and the *OED*.

Tittynope, a small quantity of anything left over, appeared in an 1896–1905 *English Dialect Dictionary*, according to *The Word Museum*.

Zythepsary, for a brewhouse, appears in *An English Dictionary* (1713), according to *The Word Museum*.

U

"What is a word to describe the process of going through the dirty-clothes hamper to find something clean enough to wear?"

—*Gail Jarocki, Richmond, Calif.*

Evidently, the behavior in question is rampant in our land. At least, an astonishing number of people who responded to this request for a word admitted they drew on personal experience. Do cultural anthropologists know about this? Do laundry-detergent marketing executives?

"Too often in the morning I find myself frantically pawing through the hamper, hoping that my mother-in-law won't come knocking at the door and catch me," Nils Jonsson, of Sugar Land, Texas, wrote. The term that Jonsson (among others) coined to describe what he does is *skivvy-dipping*. "My husband *snifferentiates* the foul shirts from the merely stale while getting dressed in the morning," Jara Kern, of New York City, wrote. Denise Mathew, of Charlottesville, Va., confessed, "In my home this process occurs weekly at least." Taking a mind-over-matter approach, she calls what she does *brainwashing*.

Here's an optimist—Jessica Chaiken, of Washington, D.C., who wrote: "According to my current theory of *laundry compost-*

ing, the heat and pressure of the top layer of clothing will clean the bottom layer. I'm still working on this theory. I'm sure there's a government grant out there somewhere!"

Here's a realist—Noel Trout, of Los Angeles, who wrote: "My wife, Cathy, and I have done our share of *snifting* while trying to find something suitable in the dirty-clothes pile (we won't even claim our dirty clothes make it into a hamper)."

Here's an intellectual—William Weaver, of New York City, who wrote: "To call it a dirty-clothes hamper is to overstate the case. For many of us, the hamper is like an overstock bin where clothes go into a complex holding pattern, and a quick *windventory* will often produce a perfectly respectable outfit."

And here's someone remembering a morning she'd probably rather forget—Amy Herzberg, of Fayetteville, Ark. She wrote: "Recently I rummaged through my laundry hamper to find something to wear to an important meeting. In the kitchen I forced my husband to sniff my armpits to ensure my secret would be safe. At that exact moment our overnight guest appeared in the doorway. We all froze. No one spoke. Then we sat down to breakfast as if nothing had happened." Herzberg's term for what she was doing is *desperspirationalizing*.

And here's someone succinctly explaining an apt, droll coinage—Jill Geisler, of Bayside, Wis. She wrote: "This process is familiar to anyone who has or has been a teenager. I believe this laundry alternative is known as **dry gleaning**."

JUST ONE THING AFTER ANOTHER

❖·❖

An idiosyncratic lexicon.

Asyou: the bottom or top step of the stairs where
things are put—from "As you go up/down take
this with you" (Faith M. Thompson, of Clare-
more, Okla., in *Family Words*). *Unexplained
Sniglets of the Universe* contains the similar
word *azugos*, defined as "items to be carried
upstairs by the next ascending person."

Beavo: a pencil with teeth marks all over it (*More
Sniglets*).

Blowers: tableware not used during a meal that
can be put back in the drawer or cupboard
without being washed (Pam Herman, of Cen-
treville, Va., in *Family Words*).

Cancuffs: the plastic ring that holds together six-
packs of beer or pop (Kevin Robart, of Moncton,
New Brunswick, in *Wanted Words 2*). According
to *Sniglets*, another name for *cancuffs* is *flan-
nister.*

Clinguini: that one strand of pasta that remains
stuck to the bottom of the pan as you're empty-
ing it into the colander (*Angry Young Sniglets*).

Delaware: the hideous stuff on the shelves of a
rented house (from *The Deeper Meaning of Liff*,
which has put the name of the American state
to this new use).

Dotsia: the name for any plant whose name you don't know (a WIOD listener, in Miami, in *Family Words*).

Finector snout: an all-purpose part name (coiner not identified, in *Family Words*).

Flathead: a species of bird that flies into picture windows (Allison Parker-Hedrick, of Virginia Beach, Va., in *Family Words*).

Forgetabilia: the opposite of memorabilia (coined by the author, editor, and radio host Clifton Fadiman, in *Family Words*).

Gleedebris: the pile of wrapping paper and ribbon left after all the gifts have been opened (*Angry Young Sniglets*).

Grubstake: the plastic bar used to divide shoppers' groceries at the checkout counter (Shirley Ring, of Seaforth, Ontario, in *Wanted Words 2*). Synonyms (also from *Wanted Words 2*) include *food fence, grocery gate*, and *provision division*. *Sniglets* proposes *spratchett*.

Ludlow: a wad of newspaper, folded table napkin, or lump of cardboard put under a wobbly table or chair to make it stand up straight (from *The Deeper Meaning of Liff*, which put the name of a nine-hundred-year-old Norman town in Shropshire, England, to a new use).

Rainbrella: "My nine-year-old daughter, Alexandra, put *rain* and *umbrella* together when she was a tot. Despite the picture appearing under the letter 'U' in her learning-to-read books, the thing was and has remained a *rainbrella*. My seven-year-old, Eryn, and two-year-old, Sophie, don't even recognize the correct word, owing mainly to the influence of their big sister" (Michael Zelek, of Canton, Mich., a reader of my Word Court newspaper column).

Sigglesthorne: anything used in lieu of a toothpick (from *The Deeper Meaning of Liff*, which borrowed the name of a village in East Riding of Yorkshire, England).

Sluce: a large slice, as in "Cut me a *sluce* of that delicious cake" (Ruth Kaminski, of Richmond, Mich., a reader of my Word Court newspaper column).

Smearisary: the part of a kitchen wall reserved for the schooltime daubings of small children (from *The Deeper Meaning of Liff*, which borrowed the name of a village in Highland, Scotland). Various Web sites assert that *The Meaning of Liff* defines *Smearisary* as "the correct name for a junior apprentice greengrocer whose main duty is to arrange the fruit so that the bad side is underneath. From the name of a character not in Dickens." It ain't so in my copy of the original book or in the revised edition, *The Deeper Meaning of Liff*. But cf. *mocteroof*, on page 161.

Snackmosphere: the empty but explosive layer of air at the top of a potato chip bag (*More Sniglets*).

Umbilinkus: the tiny appendage at the end of a link sausage (*More Sniglets*).

Wijjicle: a perverse household article, always out of order (*Burgess Unabridged*).

Zeppelingerie: undergarments for the full-figured frau (Frank Mullen III, of Aledo, Ill., in The Style Invitational).

❧·❦

U

"I'd like a word to denote the tendency of traffic to cluster around and behind highway patrol cars on rural interstates because no one dares to pass the trooper vehicle at a significant speed (that is, the speed at which the car was traveling before it caught up with the patrol car). I commute daily through rural Iowa and see this occur frequently."

—*Bruce Gelder, Iowa City, Iowa*

Not only can you neologize this time, but also you can take your pick of existing below-the-dictionary-radar terms. Michael Slancik, of Kalamazoo, Mich., wrote: "When I look in the rearview mirror of my patrol car and see that traffic cluster, I, like most of us 'on the job,' refer to it as *V'd up*. Some of us are also goose hunters and use the term for geese flying in V-formation." Gerard Farrell, of Navasota, Texas, wrote, "I can't speak to the drivers' tendencies, but in this state we refer to the police vehicle itself as a *rolling roadblock*." According to Alan Fryar, of Lexington, Ky., though, that's backward. Fryar wrote, "My cousin, a former Kentucky state policeman, referred to the tendency of traffic to stagnate behind him on I-75 as a *rolling roadblock*."

Jim Reid, of Guelph, Ontario, wrote: "As coincidence would have it, on my way to buy a copy of the magazine that had this question in it, I found myself suddenly braking with a string of other cars as a police cruiser appeared from a dirt side road. It then held us grimly at the speed limit. *Skidlock* describes the immediate response to a police car." And Mark Penney, of West Lafayette, Ind., says that in the environs of the Indianapolis 500, "for obvious reasons we refer to this as the *pace-car phenomenon*."

I love the word that Sam P. Allen, of Toledo, Ohio, and Naples, Fla., submitted to describe "the human condition that prevents motorists from passing a police patrol car": *arrestlessness*. As for the people who hang back behind a patrol car, some designate them *road worriers*. A term that lots of people came up with is *cruiser control*. Then again, we could give new meaning to the term *ticketless travel* (Patricia Chu, of Houston). Or what about *slowest common speedometer* (Jerome Kamer, of Los Angeles)? Alas, those terms don't do the job requested: describing the tendency.

One that does was suggested by several people, including Kurt Sauer, of Bethesda, Md., who said he learned it from listening to police officers when he worked as a paramedic, and Frank Williams, of Tempe, Ariz., who learned it from a former director of the Arizona Department of Public Safety. But Dan Schechter, of Los Alamitos, Calif., explained it best. Schechter wrote: "Some California Highway Patrol officers call the phenomenon the **halo effect**. The term has a double meaning: the drivers suddenly behave like angels, and the angels form an annoying halo around the patrol car."

According to dictionaries, however, *halo effect* has just one meaning, and it means something else: "generalization from the perception of one outstanding personality trait to an overly favorable evaluation of the whole personality," as *Merriam-Webster's Collegiate* explains it. But the term seems perfectly capable of multitasking without causing any confusion. Let's be supportive as it attempts to take on a wider role.

"The verb *to dial* in reference to the telephone seems antiquated already, and it will only become more obscure in ori-

gin as rotary phones go from scarcity to extinction. We need a good neologism to replace it."

—*Harriet Reisen, Arlington, Mass.*

As if you hadn't noticed by now, not all word-fugitive hunters unquestioningly do as they're told. Many who are asked to invent a replacement for the verb *dial* choose to do something else instead. Some point out that words such as *enter*, *press*, *punch in*, and *touch* are already used as synonyms for *dial*. They may add grouchy comments like "*Dial* has probably already become meaningless, but we don't need a neologism." Other people prefer to defend *dial*, even if the word is no longer strictly accurate. Bill Myer, of Kinnelon, N.J., drew an analogy: "We still call playing cards and credit cards *cards* even though they're made of plastic, but *card* comes from a root meaning 'leaf' or 'papyrus.'" Jack Miles, of Pasadena, Calif., wrote: "I frankly hope that *dial* will survive. Why deprive future generations of the fun of reading its etymology?"

Lisa Stefano, of East Boston, Mass., wrote to boast that she actually has a rotary phone, which her husband rescued from a Dumpster. She continued: "One day I was using the phone (*dialing*!) and one of my daughter's little friends, four years old, poked her head into the room in alarm, demanding an explanation of the noise I was making. Truthfully, I usually walk around the house with my cordless headset phone. When I use my headset phone, I am not *dialing* numbers but *calling* them."

WHAT *ARE* THESE WORDS?

What did *The Washington Post's* Style Invitational ask readers to do to come up with them?

ATOYOT: a mysterious brand of car visible only from your rearview mirror (proposed by Marty McCullen, of Gettysburg, Pa., and Russell Beland, of Springfield, Va.)

Citoruen: a car marketed to the overanxious (Richard Grantham, of Melbourne, Australia)

Dopi: the dwarf who walked around with wires hanging out of his ears (Lennie Magida, of Potomac, Md.)

Elppin: a shy little creature that becomes visible only when cold (Tom Witte, of Montgomery Village, Md.)

Onisac: a dark, often smoke-filled chamber in which elderly *Homo sapiens* deposit their nest eggs before dying (Peter Metrinko, of Plymouth, Minn.)

Ottelits: the depressions made in carpets by high heels (Richard Grantham, of Melbourne, Australia)

Saib: a make of car that is pulled over frequently for no apparent reason (Tom Witte, of Montgomery Village, Md.)

YMRA: a place where you can fight with the boys, you can have a meal ready to eat, you can do anything you're told; just don't tell us you're gay (Mike Connaghan, of Alexandria, Va.)

THEY ARE . . .

. . . some of the results when The Style Invitational challenged readers to spell an existing word backward and "redefine it, somehow relating the definition to the original word."

Other people responding to this question invoked words from foreign languages, or submitted English words used in a particular part of the world or of our country. "German helps us out with *wählen*, translated as *select* or *choose*," Fred Rosenberg, of Westlake Village, Calif., wrote. *Compose*, cognate with the word used in French, was suggested by several people, among them Oleh Havrylyshyn, of Rockville, Md., who wrote, "This usage would delight the Académie française, since more borrowings have gone in the other direction." Several people pointed out that people in Britain say *ring*.

And four separately wrote about a southern regionalism. Obviously, this isn't something they coined; in fact, it appears in the *Dictionary of American Regional English*. All the same, it's a fine word. Let's have Ed Ringness, of Seattle, introduce it. Once, on a business trip to Raleigh, N.C., Ringness was having trouble with his rental car, he wrote, "and a friendly taxi driver stopped to let me use his cellular phone." The driver, explaining how to make a call, "used the word **mash** in place of *dial* or *press*—as in **mash** your number, then **mash** 'send.' "

U

"There is a traffic light that is always red when I approach from one direction on the way to work, but when I approach from a different direction on the way home, it is always red in that direction. What is the word for this ability of a traffic light to sense my approach and turn red, knowing it is me?"

—*Andy Paleologopoulos, Longmeadow, Mass.*

Here's another phenomenon that skeptics argue doesn't need a new name. But in this case, it's because they decide it's not worth naming. For instance, Scott Barolo, of Ann Arbor, Mich., wrote, snarkily, "I believe I can diagnose the belief that traffic patterns revolve around oneself: *carcissism*."

Most people, though, are willing to go along with the idea that a traffic light might have paranormal powers. M. Vincenzo Scrimenti, of Erie, Pa., wrote: "Sometimes if I run through a yellow light for which I probably should have stopped, upon returning to that light I notice this phenomenon. I believe that the light thinks I have undermined its authority, and it becomes *self-lighteous*." Derek P. Pullan, of Heber City, Utah, wrote: "When I was a teenager, I worked two summers in the traffic division of the county public-works department. With this vast experience, I suggest the following word: *semaphoreknowledge*."

Holly Folk, of Bloomington, Ind., wrote to say that she thinks "a conscious (and malicious?) traffic light is *claret-voyant*." Rick Blanco, of Warwick, R.I., suggested, "The traffic light senses *bad carma*."

But here's a simple and elegant coinage from Max Frankel, of New York City: **redribution**.

U

"What do you call the phenomenon wherein a mechanical or electronic device, having gone on the blink, resumes working perfectly while the repair person examines it, and then goes kaput again once you're out of reach of the person who can repair it?"

—Phil Miller, Denver

Might that be *devious ex machina* or *deus hex machina*? Or *afixia*, *refixcidivism*, or *rekaputulation*? *On the wink*? *Hocus operandi*? More than one person sent in each of these.

Dirk Vanderloop, of Chico, Calif., didn't feel the need to get fancy. He wrote: "The condition described is all too familiar to me as a former automotive and aerospace technician. The official industrial term is *intermittent failure*." And Jeff Abbas, of Minneapolis, advised, "Inconsistent malfunctions in machinery are known as *gremlins*." Sure enough, the *American Heritage Dictionary* gives the definition "an imaginary gnomelike creature to whom mechanical problems, especially in aircraft, are attributed."

To Michael Deskey, of New York City, the phenomenon called to mind a funny story. Deskey sent me a photocopy of a chapter of the 1963 book *A Short History of Fingers and Other State Papers*, by H. Allen Smith, so that I could read it for myself. In 1936 an NBC radio engineer named Claude Fetridge attempted to broadcast, live, the flight of the swallows from Mission San Juan Capistrano, in California. Unfortunately, that year the swallows skipped out of San Juan Capistrano on October 22, a day earlier than tradition calls for, and a lot of personnel and equipment arrived just in time to record . . . nothing in particular. How does this relate? In H. Allen Smith's words, "*Fetridge's Law*, in simple language, states that important things that are supposed to happen do not happen, especially when people are looking or, conversely, things that are supposed to *not* happen do happen, especially when people are looking."

RUSTLED UP

The writer and editor Anne Fadiman, when asked to share a few words, chose her family's names for things, along with her thoughts about them:
Many families, I think, use words coined by young children whose

vocabularies are still malleable and imaginative. Most of those words are mispronunciations of "real" words, like the *Train of Cold Meat Tessa* (Train à Grande Vitesse)—a splendid term coined by our son, Henry, when he was in his railroad phase at age three, and one that's still in service in our family today. We're not so glamorous that three-year-old Henry learned about the TGV by experience; there was a picture of it in a train book of which he was particularly fond. But we're going to France this summer and are looking forward to taking the Train of Cold Meat Tessa from Paris to Bordeaux.

Sometimes the words are entirely new. When our daughter, Susannah, was two, she accompanied us to a secondhand furniture store where we shopped for a swiveling desk chair for my study. After twirling around delightedly in a dozen chairs, she announced, "I love *introducety* chairs!" Where did this word come from? She's fifteen now and hasn't a clue (though the last two syllables—pronounced "doose-ty"—have always sounded onomatopoetically *roll*-y to me).

To this day, in the Fadiman & Colt household, *introducety* is the preferred adjective for any swivel chair. Why did this term stick? It's not a word invented to fit a previously unmet need; rather, it's part of our family's secret language—a bit of glue that, because it's familiar only to us, helps to bind us together.

And Samuel Jay Keyser, an M.I.T. professor emeritus of linguistics and a professional trombone player, has a word for, um, a particular kind of thing-ification:

The pyramids in Egypt and the temple at Angkor Wat built for Suryavarman II in Cambodia—what do they have in common? They share the conceit that the soul of the dead lives on in the stone. That hard gray gilded edifice is not merely tufa or granite. It is the abstract become concrete, the ineffable expressed, the soul in the stone.

It is hard to know who needed this conceit more: the king who ordered his own memorial or the priest who attended him. Immortality was at stake for the king. For the priest, it was his livelihood. While the king was alive, the priest thrived on his living presence. But kings do not live forever. The problem was how to make the beat go on when the drummer left town. The answer seemed simple: Don't let him leave. Let the stone become the soul. We need a word for this. I suggest *incairnation*.

Incairnation is a big idea. It is no accident that kings, priests, medicine men, writers, composers, artists of all stripes, have taken it up. After all, *incairnation* is precisely what happened to the Earth. The Earth was a stone that became imbued with life. The *incairnators* of history were trying to replicate that ancient magic act.

STILL AT LARGE

 Here are a few material-world fugitives that as yet elude our grasp.

"I seek a word or phrase to describe a cheap plastic thing that is better for a task than its expensive metal counterpart."

—*Brett Gibson, Concrete, Wash.*

"What's the word for the fizz that goes above the rim of a cup of soda?"

—*Ethan Bendheim*

"My daughter and I were discussing this the other day: We had each bought the same shoulder bag, but it turned out that it kept slipping off our shoulders. You would say this bag was . . . ?"

—*Doris Fleischman, Albany, N.Y.*

"What would you call the experience of seeing something in the real, like a painting, after having been familiar with it only in reproductions? This is a common and profound event that I don't know how to refer to."

—*Nick de Matties, Phoenix*

"We need a word for food that hasn't quite gone bad—the things you aren't sure whether you ought to throw them out."

—Anne Bernays and Justin Kaplan, Cambridge, Mass.

"In Russian there is a word for 'a construction project started, but not completed—usually owing to lack of funds.' Don't we need a similar word in English?"

—Kim Fisher, San Francisco

"Is there a word for it when the sea and the sky blend together because of clouds and you can't see the horizon?"

—Willa Bluebird, Bumpas, Va.

4

TRIBULATIONS

Granted, the annoyances in this chapter are petty. But that's no reason to suffer them in silence. Complaining is cathartic—except when it's poorly received. Then suffering tends to beget suffering. When you regale friends with a tale of woe and what you get back is what you should have done to avoid the problem, that's unsatisfying. It's a tribulation in itself.

Another unsatisfying response is a puzzled look and a put-down like "You let that kind of stuff upset you?" Or else someone might say, "Oh, yes, that happened to me once too . . . ," and launch into an irrelevant anecdote, leaving you feeling misunderstood as well as un-unburdened. Or sometimes the listener might put a name to what happened to you, summing up your whole story in a word or phrase: "So you got a hangover." "You tripped." "Oh—a flat tire!"

Unless the comment is followed up with sympathy, naming the problem tends to imply "Heard *that* one before. Ho-hum."

A bit better is when the person says, "That happened to me," and then tells a story relevant to the one you just told. This may not be sympathy, but it can pass for empathy. Rapt, concerned sympathy is the best, but it's rare. We are, after all, just talking about petty annoyances.

In my experience, most of the fun, or the catharsis, in sharing tribulations lies in how you tell your tale. And somehow, if you yourself are able to put a name to what happened—preferably a name no one else has heard before—*this* can be satisfying. You have been afflicted by something special, possibly unique. So much the better if you can make a joke out of it.

In this spirit, shall we accept that life is hell—or at any rate, annoying? Let's try to enjoy it anyway.

U

"We need a word for those periods in which every little thing that can go wrong does—orders get lost, the wrong washing machine is delivered, your ATM card is eaten, and so forth."
—*Jan Freeman, Brookline, Mass.*

Many people, when thinking about this fugitive, think of Murphy's Law. Although this is usually stated as "Anything that can go wrong will," it's occasionally expressed in terms of the inevitability that falling toast will land buttered-side down. *Murph*, *murphase*, and *Murphy moment* were among the suggestions received.

People of more idiosyncratic turns of mind came up with *chagrinterval* (J. Robert Lennon, of Ithaca, N.Y.), *fluster cluster* (Charles Memminger, of Honolulu), *awry spell* (Connie West, of Cincinnati), and *bad err day* (Gina Loebell, of East Windsor, N.J.). Ilan Kinsley, of Sioux Falls, S.D., came up with an entire week's worth of possibilities: "*Mournday, Bluesday, Winceday, Curseday, Frightday,* and, of course, *the Bleakend.*" Jennifer Lewis, of New Orleans, wrote: "A natural-born klutz, I tend to regularly experience the phenomenon described. Sometimes my life seems one big, bumbling *calamitime.*"

But perhaps the most productive line of thought was *karma* combinations. For instance, *karmageddon* (Chris Nauyokas, of Chicago) and—better yet—**karmaclysm** (Miko Dwarkin, of Calgary, Alberta).

"We need a word that means 'a problem caused by a blundering or heavy-handed attempt to cure another problem.' Examples include parties at off-campus apartments because eighteen-year-olds aren't allowed to drink in bars, and

groundwater contaminated with MTBE, which is put in
gasoline to reduce pollution."

—*David F. Wilson, Stamford, N.Y.*

Such a problem might be called a *boomerwrong* (Pat Bergeson, of
Chicago), a *blunderang* (Joel Hess, of Portland, Ore.), or maybe a
solut—"a little short of a solution," as David Israel, of Santa Clara,
Calif., explained his word.

Idiotrogenic (Michaele Dunlap, of Lake Oswego, Ore.) is nice,
but it's an adjective, not a noun, as requested, and the related noun
form, *idiotrogenesis*, is awfully fancy. Two promising possibilities
are *ouchcome* and *oopshot* (both from M. S. Coats, of Oregon City,
Ore.).

Some people supplemented their coinages with examples. Jim
Felde, of Concord, Calif., mentioned "attempting to pull out a
tree stump by tying a rope to the car's bumper and thereby
wrenching the latter from the vehicle" in the course of proposing
fixasco.

Richard Leeman, of Scotts Valley, Calif. (what is it with West
Coasters and this fugitive?), told a story from his childhood: "On
a cold winter day in Milwaukee, when our frozen car wouldn't
start, my father laid some tarred hemp (oakum) on the ground under the engine and lit it. Within a couple of minutes the entire engine was ablaze." Leeman's suggested coinage was *delution*—an
invention so similar in pronunciation to an existing word that if

spoken it would surely be misunderstood, thereby exemplifying the very problem for which a name is being sought.

As it happens, this was the case with a number of suggestions received, including *solvo* (Andy Hirth, of Columbia, Mo.) and *botchulism, dissolution* or *dyssolution*, and *wrecktification* (all suggested by several people). Maria Rhew, of Shady Hills, Fla., however, in lobbying for her coinage, cleverly explained away this shortcoming by making the case that it is actually an advantage. "Not only is it apropos," she wrote, "but the potential confusion created by its pronunciation would continually contribute to the very need for its existence!" I'll buy that. Her term is ***side defect.***

U

"I'm a good speller, and a good typist. I'm also very good at math: I've been a professional statistician for thirty-plus years. My problem is that I'm terrible at transcribing numbers. To make a phone call, I have to put my finger on the number in the book and refer to it several times while dialing. Is there a word for my affliction?"

—Tim Carr, Atlanta

The closest English that previously came to an appropriate word for the disorder was *dyscalculia*—but that means "difficulty in solving math problems." And *dysnumia* probably shouldn't become a word, because it's too much like the medical term *dysnomia*, which means "difficulty in finding the right word or words."

Some people think the right word is *fourgetfulness*. Others like *digititis*. Sharon S. Tonjes, of DeLand, Fla., wrote, "To borrow a term from my computer keyboard, your correspondent has a bad case of *num lock*." But an even better suggestion is **dialexia**—submitted by six people, the first of whom was Emily Pepe, of Portland, Ore.

Evidently, whatever you choose to call it, this condition afflicts many people. If you're among them, you may be interested in a couple of suggestions about how to cope. James E. Hunter, of Camden, S.C., advised, "The difficulty can be solved by repeating the offending telephone number ALOUD." Karen Kwa, of Hong Kong, wrote: "The problem: keypads on calculators and telephones are upside-down left-right images of each other. I can use a calculator blindly throughout the day to key in numbers with few errors, so for me, one partial solution is to hold the phone the other way around, such that the bottom of the keypad is now at the top."

U

"What is the word to describe the moment right before you are about to do something terribly stupid, when everything

A LITTLE CROP OF HORRORS

This lexicon of tribulations consists of four dictionary words (mostly archaic, rare, or dialectal), and twelve words of the kind this book is mainly about, including four Liff words. Which are which?

Acle: the pin that shirtmakers conceal in a fold of a new shirt, so as to stab you when you try the shirt on

Barfium: the horrible-smelling cleanser they mop down school corridors with

Black cow: an imaginary black cow said to tread on one when calamity comes

Faux-matoes: those out-of-season, cardboard-tasting tomatoes we get in restaurants in the winter

Furbling: having to wander through a maze of ropes at an airport or bank even when you are the only person in line

Gallinipper: a large mosquito

Goslip: the wrong tale carried to the wrong person

Gungus: the stuff on a three-year-old's hands

Henstridge: a dried yellow substance found between the prongs of forks in restaurants

Malindropity: serendipity's negative counterpart; a bad coincidence

Nantucket: the secret pocket that eats your train ticket

Ogerhunch: any frightful or loathsome creature, especially a bat

Pulicosity: an abundance of, or being full of, fleas

Rocktose: the hard lumps that block the pouring spouts of sugar dispensers

Tananarive: to announce your entrance by falling over the dustbin in the drive

Yard ape: overly active mischievous child who tends to do less damage outside than in

THE HORRORS REVEALED

Whence this repellent miscellany.

Acle is actually the name of a village in Norfolk, England, where bird-watching is a popular leisure-time activity. *The Deeper Meaning of Liff* misappropriated the name to mean a rogue pin in a shirt.

Barfium, a repulsive cleanser, appears in *Unexplained Sniglets of the Universe*.

That spectral *black cow* appears in *The Scottish National Dictionary* (1931–41), according to *The Word Museum*.

Faux-matoes was coined by Anne Drake, of Ann Arbor, Mich., a reader of my Word Court newspaper column.

Furbling, for wandering among the ropes, appears in *Sniglets*.

Gallinipper, for a large mosquito, appears in *Weird and Wonderful Words* and the *Oxford English Dictionary*.

Goslip, ill-advised gossip, appears in *Not the Webster's Dictionary*.

Gungus, for grunge, was coined by Kelly Courtney, of Pittsfield, Mass.

Henstridge, for stuff between a fork's prongs, appears in *The Deeper Meaning of Liff*. Otherwise, it is a village in Somerset, England.

Malindropity, a bad coincidence, was coined by Russ Harvey, of Cody's Books, in Berkeley, Calif.

Nantucket designates a pocket in *The Deeper Meaning of Liff*, but of course, in reality it is the name of an island off Massachusetts.

Ogerhunch, a loathsome bat, comes from *A Glossary of the Shetland and Orkney Dialect* (1866), according to *The Word Museum*.

Pulicosity, the state of being flea-ridden, comes from *The Royal English Dictionary* (1775), according to *The Word Museum*.

Rocktose, for lumpy sugar, appears in *Sniglets*.

Tananarive, for a clumsy arrival, appears in *The Deeper Meaning of Liff*. Otherwise, it's an old French name for Antananarivo, the capital of Madagascar.

Yard ape, meaning "mischievous child," was coined by Matthew and Daniel Sissman, of Latham, N.Y., and appears in *Family Words*.

runs in slow motion? The actions I mean include watching hopelessly as you lock your keys in the car, knock over a beverage at dinner, or insert a stack of bills into the mailbox—including the checks you had intended to take to the bank for deposit."

—*Deborah Ro, Seattle*

This is another word that many people have need of, as these examples of situations that cry out for such a word demonstrate.

David Noller, of Burbank, Calif., wrote: "I once was absentmindedly dangling my arm out the fully open window of my car—until a moment of awareness that lasted a millisecond before the automated carwash nozzle began to fire at high velocity one foot from my face."

Jeanne Flavin, of New York City, reported that she "once slammed down the child-proof cap onto a large bottle of Tylenol, catching the web of my hand between the lid and the bottle, with the lid in the locked position." She then "desperately searched for a way to pry it off, during which entire time the bottle of pills was shaking like a maraca."

And Henry Evans, D.M.D., of Chewelah, Wash., wrote: "As a young orderly, I once observed a physician accidentally squirt a large amount of antiseptic soap into a patient's eye, thinking he was using a sterile saline rinse. I knew he was going to do it and that it was wrong before it happened, but it was too late to stop him or even to say anything."

As you may recall, word fugitives about all sorts of things tend to elicit plays on *déjà vu*. This one was déjà vu all over again: Several people suggested *déjà rue* or *déjà fou*; Bill Parton, of Russellville, Ark., *dejaphooey*; and yet other people proposed *déjà* expressions too impolite to print. A number of *Simpsons* fans also wrote in, invoking Homer's deathless *D'oh!* and variants thereof. A few people even blended the two notions. For instance, Matt Breaden, of Lake Oswego, Ore., wrote, "I am a longtime fan of *The Simpsons*, and so, the moment before doing something stupid, I often feel a profound sense of *deja d'oh*."

Suggestions that lack any particular cultural referents include *pregret*, a popular coinage; *dunderstruck* (Jon Miller, of New Haven, Conn.); *slipupiphany* (Kenneth Tishgart, of Ross, Calif.); and, particularly to describe "a social blunder," *time-lapse faux pas–graphy* (Paul Liversage, of Fargo, N.D.).

All well and good, but it was Tim Sargent, of Keams Canyon, Ariz., who hit the nail on the, um, thumb? He wrote: "An all-encompassing term for these moments of stopeless hupidity might be ***instant regretification***."

U

"Like many urbanites, I stand in line many times during the day, such as when eating lunch in a fast-food outlet. When I

stand in line, I always think that the line next to me is moving faster. That is what usually happens. Can you help me with a word to describe my thinking?"

—*Arvin V. Reyes, Quezon City, the Philippines*

OK, is such an observer delusional or bravely facing the truth? People who are thinking about this word fugitive tend to get sidetracked trying to decide.

Richard Bagby, of Las Cruces, N.M., wrote: "If two persons simultaneously enter lines of equal length, the one in the slower line spends more time there. So on average, a significantly greater fraction of the time spent waiting in lines is spent in slow-moving lines than in fast-moving lines." Joe Touch, of Manhattan Beach, Calif., wrote: "Often thinking the line next to you is moving faster is called *statistics*. Consider your line, the one to your left, and the one to your right as a set of three. The chance that you will be in the fastest line, all other things being equal, is one in three, or 33 percent." And Nathan Perez, of Chapel Hill, N.C., invoked Einstein's theory of relativity before explaining: "The line you are in appears slower because when you look ahead, your movement equals that of those in your line. For all intents and purposes, you are not moving at all. A possible term might be *express relativism*: when you are in the express lane, it is no longer express."

Several people pointed out that the relevant principle has already been named *Ettore's Observation* (after Barbara Ettore, a business writer). This even has a corollary: If you switch lines, the line you were in will begin moving faster.

Others, who are looking for a neologism, find the common American word *line* a less thought-provoking starting point than its primarily British English equivalent, *queue*. For instance, the term we're looking for might be *misqueue* or *disqueuetude* (both popular suggestions). Or it could be *a queue anxiety* (Alan Horoschak, of Sitka, Alaska), a *persequeuetion complex* (Russ Hurd, of Copley, Ohio), *piqueue* (Bernard Goldhirsch, of East Hampton, N.Y.), *unluqueuey* (Fran M. Grove-White, of Toronto, Ontario), *queueriosity* (Jeffrey J. Forster, of Pittsburgh), or *quevetousness* (Geoffrey Andersen, of Oakland, Calif.).

But let's go with **misalinement** (Glenn Thomsen, of Appleton, Wis.). Not only is this a down-to-earth, American coinage, but it does double duty as a word for standing in an objectively slower line and as a word for the unverified observation that one seems to be doing so.

U

"My wife and I have been searching for a term that describes the manner in which two people who dislike each other manage to avoid acknowledgment, even in close proximity, when their paths cross in public."

—*Carson Stanwood, Jackson Hole, Wyo.*

Troy Bramston, of Sydney, Australia, wrote, "This is what is known as giving each other the *cold shoulder*." True—but what fun is that?

Chris Lazzarino, of Lawrence, Kan., apparently had no trouble getting into the spirit of the question. He wrote: "Ah, the delight in seeing and not acknowledging your spiteful, black-hearted little enemy! Few dark pleasures are more satisfying than dishing out the *silent greetment*." Lisa Crocker, of Springfield, Ill., had a suggestion that, she admitted, "is more like a non-greeting." Her word is *hellno*.

Further possibilities include *circumnavihate* (Katie Fife, of Dallas), *n'approchement* (Jerry Schoen, of New Salem, Mass.), *snide-stepping* (Pamela Halverson, of Raleigh, N.C.), and *unanimosity* (Pat Geoghegan, of Montreal, Quebec). Pamela Stewart, of Grand Rapids, Mich., wrote: "Two people avoiding each other in a social situation? Each is, to the other, a *persona non greeta*."

Or how about *near-dis* (David Hochman, of Santa Monica, Calif.) or *sneer miss* (Nancy Lewkowicz, of Yellow Springs, Ohio)? Or *proxenmity* (Stephen Zender, of Hudson, Wis.) or *close poxenmity* (James H. Ballard, of West Lebanon, N.H.). Or *snubterfuge* (Clela Reed, of Athens, Ga.) or *snubbing their foes* (P. Pagan, of Santa Barbara, Calif.).

What an embarrassment of riches! But I think the cleverest correspondent on this subject was Karen Sparapani, of Wauwatosa, Wis., whose coinage is ***can't-standoffish***.

U

"I would like a word for my tendency to make more mistakes, even doing familiar things like writing a check or slicing bread, if a very critical person is watching."

—*Helen S. Sharpe, Albany, N.Y.*

This tendency is evidently a common one: along with aspiring words, descriptions of what it's like to be afflicted poured in. For instance, Peter Morris, of Swarthmore, Pa., wrote, "I often find myself unable to sign my own name when being stared at by an incommunicative bank teller or bureaucrat." Javan Kienzle, of Birmingham, Mich., wrote: "It is near impossible for me to work in the kitchen if anyone else is in there—this from my childhood when my mother always commented on the way I did things. If anyone watches me work, I inevitably end up cutting myself, burning myself, dropping something, or breaking something."

Two people reported that according to *They Have a Word for It*, by Howard Rheingold, in German *fisselig* has the meaning wanted ("flustered to the point of incompetence"). A few others pointed out that among sports fans, *choke* nearly fills the bill. But, naturally, people coined many new terms too. Some of these, though clever, were for the state or process or cause or effect of bungling under supervision rather than for the tendency to bungle, as requested. For instance, *abutter-fingers* (Rita Kennedy, of Rockland, Mass.), *botchful eye* (Rebecca Cosgrove, of New Milford, Conn.), and *bungle of nerves* (Vera K. Cobb, of Ipswich, Mass.). Hitting closer to the target were *sage fright* (a popular suggestion), *glarer-prone* (Lynn Herrick, of Northville, Mich.), *stuporvised* (Patrick Green, of Dripping Springs, Texas), and *tsk-oriented* (Art Scherer, of Efland, N.C.). Jim Tanner, of Fort Collins, Colo., wrote, "I tend to become particularly witless while pursuing tasks in the presence of a critical witness; hence my witlessness is compounded—hence *witnesslessness.*"

And here's a winner: **carper-fumble syndrome** (David Sonstroem, of Storrs, Conn.).

U

"How about a word for that dicey moment when you should introduce two people but can't remember one of their names?"

—*Judith Kelman, New York City*

Michael Huston, of Joplin, Mo., wrote, archly: "A strange word indeed. If it really must be a word for 'that dicey moment,' then I have no entry. However, it seems that *whomnesia* is the word for the introducer's affliction." Good point, Michael. It *wasn't* clear whether the wanted word should describe the moment per se, what one might perform instead of an introduction, or one's state of mind in that dicey moment. Therefore we'll accept anything halfway relevant.

For instance, *persona non data* (Susan K. Costello, of New York City) and *nomstruck* (Peter Anderson, of Joliet, Ill.). Carolyn Coleburn, of Ridgefield, Conn., wrote: "May I suggest *nomenclutchure*? It happens to me all the time." Josh Dodes, of Burlington, Vt., wrote, "If meeting people and making introductions is the key to successful networking, this is clearly *notworking*."

Or possibly "that dicey moment" is a *mumbleduction* (Patty Namm, of New York City), an *introdeduction* (Barbara Jacobs, of Medfield, Mass.), an *introdiction* (Bonnie Brueckner, of La Jolla, Calif.), or an *ain'troduction* (Emily Etheridge, of Louisville, Ky.).

But who has really come to grips with our admittedly vaguely defined idea? Peter Gaffney, of Los Angeles, invented a pair of coinages that together cover the possibilities pretty well. Gaffney wrote: "If you weasel out of the situation by contriving to get someone else to provide the names, it's **introducking**. **Introduping** is giving the appearance of making an introduction without actually so doing."

U

"This seems to happen frequently. One says in an e-mail message that one is attaching some document or file and then

A GALLERY OF BAD BEHAVIOR

Match the words with their definitions. For extra-credit points, identify the three dictionary words that have crept in among the fugitives.

1. To complain in a whining voice	*Bindle*
2. Fakery or deceit	*Blamestorming*
3. To give unnecessary advice; one who thus bores	*Flount*
4. To go to pieces, to become highly upset	*Fringle*
5. A meeting whose sole purpose is to discuss why a deadline was missed or a project failed and who was responsible	*Glumsiness*
6. To nag the driver to the correct destination	*Hookum-snivey*
7. To rumple, crease. If one female sits so close to another as to rumple or crease her dress by pressing or sitting upon it, she is said to——it.	*Miscomfrumple*
8. To scorn, mock, or defy in a particularly conspicuous, egregious, or melodramatic manner	*Naggagate*
9. To shudder or wriggle involuntarily because of an embarrassing remark or thought, or the movement itself	*Paloodle*
10. To slip foreign coins into a customer's change	*Peenge*
11. The tendency to drop or break things when one is in a depressed mood	*Squidgel*
12. "We have a large, goofy German shepherd named Cyrus who occasionally thinks he's a lap dog. He methodically joins us on the couch, climbing over us and any books or magazines in his path. He plops down in the middle of his well-orchestrated chaos and groans happily. The verb we use to describe this mayhem is——."	*Stomple*

OWNING UP

Here's what was coined or found, and where.

1. *Peenge*, to complain in a whining voice, appears in *More Weird and Wonderful Words* and the *OED*.

2. *Hookum-snivey*, meaning "fakery or deceit," also appears in *More Weird and Wonderful Words* and the *OED*.

3. *Paloodle*, to give unnecessary advice or one who thus bores, is an invented word that appears in *Burgess Unabridged*.

4. The family word *fringle* was defined as "to go to pieces" by Jessica Buster, of Fairly, Vt., on *All Things Considered* in July of 1995.

5. *Blamestorming* was defined as a meeting "to discuss why a deadline was missed or a project failed and who was responsible" by Dany Levy in *The New York Times Magazine*, August 22, 2004.

6. *Naggagate*, to nag the driver to the correct destination, was coined by Joyce Rudder, of Warren, Mich., a reader of my Word Court newspaper column.

7. *Miscomfrumple* is defined as "to rumple, crease" in *The English Dialect Dictionary* (1896–1905), according to *The Word Museum*.

8. *Flount*, to scorn, mock, or defy conspicuously or melodramatically, was coined by the journalist Daniel Schorr for *In a Word*. Schorr explained, "*Flount* ends the confusion of *flaunt* and *flout* once and for all."

9. *Squidgel*, meaning "to shudder or wriggle involuntarily," was coined by Geraldine Hurley, of the Berkshires, Mass.

10. *Bindle* is defined as "to slip foreign coins into a customer's change" in *The Deeper Meaning of Liff*. In reality, it is the name of a hamlet (estimated population 18) in east-central Australia.

11. *Glumsiness*, the tendency to drop or break things when depressed, was coined by the poet Jane Hirshfield for *In a Word*.

12. *Stomple*, "a combination of *stomp* and *trample*," is what Cyrus the German shepherd does. The word was coined by Phyllis Sweers, of Grand Rapids, Mich., a reader of my Word Court newspaper column.

hits the 'send' button before remembering to attach the file. What would be a term for this?"

—*Katherine Bryant, Cambridge, Mass.*

Sends of omission and *e-mnesia* are popular suggestions. Other possibilities are *absentee-mail* (Richard Siegelman, of Plainview, N.Y.), *nonsendquitur* (Teri Viray, of San Diego), and *deficit sending* (Barbara Olsen, of Poughkeepsie, N.Y.).

Or what about *sentropy*, suggested by Carissa Wodehouse, of Portland, Ore.? She explained, "The definition of *entropy* in chemistry is the amount of thermal energy not available to do work, but dictionaries also give the meaning 'a measure of the loss of information in a transmitted message.'"

Another popular suggestion was ***forgetfileness***. One of the many people to suggest it was Erik Bleich, of Middlebury, Vt., who also explained it and supplied a bonus word. Bleich wrote: "In all my years of using e-mail, I never once failed to attach a promised document. I prided myself on this point. Then I read your column. The very next day, I suffered my first case of ***forgetfileness***. At least now I have a memorable term for when I forget." And his postscript: "If the oversight is of little consequence, it is mere *forgetfileness*. If it has serious repercussions, it is best called a *docudrama*."

P.S.: An idea that occurred to many, many people who thought about this fugitive was *premature dissemination* or some similar play on you know what. Well! In the conclusion to this book, you'll read about my aversion to coinages derived from clinical sexology talk. No matter what the word fugitive is, someone always thinks *premature something-ation* or *something-us interruptus* is apt and oh-so-clever. Usually it is not. At all. A pun alludes to something apropos, but mostly these coinages are, instead, irrelevant allusions. The only reason anyone might find them funny is that they refer to something naughty.

With this e-mail fugitive, though, for once *premature something-ation* actually was a pun. Even I thought it was kind of funny. But high school English teachers sometimes assign their students to coin words in response to my Word Fugitives column. I just couldn't bear to imagine the follow-up discussions in class if I pursued the *premature something-ation* line of thought in print. Never mind that among the student essays one teacher sent me, a (male) student proposed *premature something-ation*. I just couldn't bear it.

P.P.S.: A number of people who sent responses to this fugitive by e-mail amused themselves by including a line like "For explanation, see attached document" but not attaching anything. Ha-ha!

U

"We've all been in the situation of walking on a sidewalk when someone coming toward us comes directly into our path. We step to one side; they step to the same side; we

move to the other side; they do too. A comical dance ensues, until someone takes the initiative to move out of the way. What should we call this?"

—*Dan Clary, Boston, Mass.*

This is one of those questions that come up again and again. It has, however, never appeared in the Word Fugitives column, because I realized early in the game that others had already chased it down. Like a man I once met who led heli-skiing expeditions across virgin snow in the Canadian Bugaboos, I don't like to ski in other people's tracks. This is not to say that I never travel where others have gone before. But where the evidence of their presence is overwhelming, I steer clear.

Among the recreational word-coining sources that have weighed in on this is *The Deeper Meaning of Liff*, which gives *Droitwich*—a borrowing of the name of a town in Worcestershire, England, that lived off its salt wells for nearly 2,000 years. *Sniglets* gives *shuggleftulation*. The writer Frank Gannon, in *In a Word*, suggested *willie pep*, to honor an eponymous prizefighter (born in 1922, in his prime in the 1950s, and nicknamed "Will o' the Wisp," for his elusiveness). And when the Wanted Words segment of the CBC radio program *This Morning* put out a call for a word to describe "the subtle dance two strangers engage in when trying to move past each other on a sidewalk or in a hallway," the responses, recorded in *Wanted Words*, included *polkadodge* (from Katie Wood, of Lively, Ontario), *avoidance* (Murray Hagen, of

Prince Albert, Saskatchewan), *bossa no va* (Adam Levin, of Toronto, Ontario), and—my favorite—***walkstrot*** (Barbara Michaelsen, of Newmarket, Ontario).

U

"If language organizes experience, then please give me a word or phrase for the frantic period of time many families experience each morning prior to leaving home."
                                                                    —*Scott Buffett, Bedford, N.H.*

Coinages that pop into many people's heads are *pandemornium* and its variant *pandemorningum*. *A.M.*-related creations are common as well—for instance, *A.M. mayhem* (a popular suggestion), *A.M.ania* (Liz Theran, of Boston), the subtle *m A.M.* (Sarah Routh, of Cleveland Heights, Ohio), and *pandA.M.onium* (Susan Montag, of St. Cloud, Minn.).

Another fruitful line of thought is breakfast-related coinages, such as *wreckfast*, *fast break*, and *scrambled legs*. Want a second helping? *Toast-haste* (John Kirwan-Taylor, of New Orleans), *Special Chaos* (Pete McPherson, of Pegram, Tenn.), and *javavoom* (Bear Braumoeller, of Roslindale, Mass.).

The showiest possibility submitted was *Around They Whirled, Inanely Dazed*; the family of J. D. Asis, of Brookline, Mass., "all being fans of Jules Verne," delights in referring to the frantic morning period this way. For widespread everyday use, though, surely a better choice is ***brood awakening*** (Nancy Pickard, of Prairie Village, Kan.).

RUSTLED UP

Although you might imagine that Patricia C. Post, of the Emily Post Institute, leads a decorous and perfectly orchestrated life, she wrote me:

Derangements. I made this word up, from the French *déranger*, "to become disordered." I quit making arrangements with people long ago. Any plan I made at 8 A.M. was in a shambles by 10 A.M.: kids left the 90-percent-of-the-grade science project at home, dog had close encounter with porcupine, husband left wallet on kitchen counter . . . I gave up, so now I make derangements instead. I expect chaos, and so am calmer and less stressed by constantly changing plans.

And the graphic designer Amy Swan wrote me:

Accidial (can be used as a noun or verb). My husband, Marty Hergert, coined it. This is what we call it when someone accidentally dials someone else from their cell phone.

I often receive such calls because my name begins with "A"

and may be the first name in someone's phone book. When a cell phone is slid into a pocket or bag and a button or two gets inadvertently pressed, it can accidentally make a call. When the call is answered on the other end, one might hear the swish swish of someone walking or a muffled conversation. One time I heard Marty's entire walk from the subway to work, including the ding of his office elevator and the usual office *Good mornings*.

There should also be a word for what one might find out during an accidial. I heard a friend and his girlfriend get into a car and go on and on about how annoying the person they had just dined with was. Imagine if that person got the accidial instead of me, or if they were talking about me instead of that person!

STILL AT LARGE

 As discussed, being able to put a name to one's problem goes a long way toward bringing a person satisfaction. Have pity on the poor souls seeking words below.

"If I tune in to a television show only twice in any twelve-month period, inevitably I manage to stumble into the same episode each time. There should be a word for this."

—*Marian Bass, Princeton, N.J.*

"My name is Todd, but throughout my life, people—both close to me and mere acquaintances—have incorrectly called me Scott. The people who do this are unrelated to one another. I mentioned this during a luncheon gathering recently, and to my surprise another person at the table claimed a similar thing happens to his wife. I figure this phenomenon must occur with sufficient frequency to warrant a name of its own. Suggestions?"

—*Todd Nichols, Shorewood, Minn.*

"What would be a term for my tendency to lose umbrellas?"
—*Jason Wong, Sacramento, Calif.*

"Could you give me a name for a jokey remark that a spouse or other family member has made once too often?"
—*Kim James, Fort Lauderdale, Fla.*

"I need a word for this: after getting no invitations to anything for months, getting two great invitations for the same evening."

—*Elizabeth French, Chicago*

"What could we call something you said you'd be glad to do but, once you start doing it, find yourself absolutely loathing?"

—*Andi Weiss, Arlington, Va.*

"My idea of hell is wandering all over a video store and not finding anything I'm in the least interested in renting. Doesn't this activity deserve to have a name?"

—Derek Polonsky, Weston, Mass.

"What about a word for grape or tomato skins stuck to the roof of your mouth or popcorn or steak sinews stuck between your teeth?"

—Justin Kaplan, Cambridge, Mass.

"I don't suppose it happens very often to many people, but I wish there was a word for when my cat inadvertently steps on one of my remotes, changing the channel on the TV, muting it, or turning it off, usually without my immediately knowing the cause."

—Michael Deskey, New York City

"Is there a term for concentrating so hard on not saying the worst possible thing in a situation that it comes out? For instance, greeting a newly mal-coiffed friend: 'Your hair!'"

—Kat Lewin, Henderson, Nev.

MAY WE HAVE A WORD?

L et's say you start thinking about words for particular mind-sets or categories of things or bad situations or whatever—and the next thing you know, you're thinking about words. Words for words, even. The spiral of mental activity (maybe you've noticed) can narrow pretty quickly. Is there a word for this—for thoughts that close in on themselves, leaving you wondering whether you were thinking about anything at all?

Words about words are undeniably ethereal. To make matters worse, many of the old words for words, or groups of them, have fallen into disuse. We as a society would be better off, I swear, if everyone knew what words like *pronoun*, *adjective*, and *preposition* mean. I believe this because I find it nearly impossible to talk about language and how it works its wonders without employing at least basic grammatical terms. If everyone had these down, we could move on to complaining that nowadays no one understands the likes of *meiosis* ("the use of understatement not to deceive, but to enhance the impression on the hearer," as H. W. Fowler explains it in his *Modern English Usage*) and *tmesis* ("separation of the parts of a compound word by another word inserted between them"—for instance, *un-freaking-believable*).

Oh, the heck with it. Let's not go there. Instead, let's go find some people who are actively looking for words for words and want our help. As you'll notice when you get to the "Still at Large" section of this chapter, quite a backlog of this kind of word fugitive awaits. We have our work cut out for us.

U

"Is there a word for mistakenly written homonyms—*your* for *you're*, and so on?"

—*Dillon Teachout, Norwich, Vt.*

What a good question! Ever fewer people seem to be able to tell those two, or *its* and *it's*, or *led* and *lead*, or *there*, *their*, and *they're*, apart. Surely such a term would earn its keep in a language that has already made room for such specific words as *protonym*, "the first person or thing to have a certain name, after which others are named"; *poecilonym*, "one of various names for the same thing";

and *anonym*, "a person whose name is not given"—such as the coiners of the *-nym* words in this paragraph, assuming these have specific coiners.

Ian Piumarta, of Versailles, France, wrote: "Grammarians and linguists alike have for many centuries been in possession of a (somewhat technical) term describing precisely this kind of syntactic substitution. It is called a *mistake*." (Or a *misteak*, or a *misstake*, as others suggested.) Lee Dawley, of South Ryegate, Vt., wrote to say that he in particular would welcome the coining of an appropriate word. He has multiple sclerosis, which forces him to use a voice-recognition computer program in order to write. He reported: "No sooner did I say *homonyms* than this malfunctioning piece of software gave me *holograms*. And what did it give me for *fugitives*? *Primitives*!"

Nononym was a popular suggestion. Some other possibilities were *errerr* (Laura Markos, of Santa Fe, N.M.), *sinonym* (Felicia Lincoln, of Kennet Square, Pa.), and *doppelklanger* (Philip Walker, of Mississauga, Ontario). John Ford, of Coquitlam, British Columbia, wrote, "Since bird-watching is called *ornithology*, why can't we call that kind of word-botching *orthinology*?"

For cleverness combined with aptness, however, nothing beat **illiteration.** Of the three people who submitted this coinage, Rocky Raab, of Ogden, Utah, was the first to do so.

U

"We desperately need a short substitute for saying either
World Wide Web **or** ***double-u double-u double-u*** **(mostly pronounced here in Texas 'dub-ya dub-ya dub-ya')! Please ad-
vise."**

—Sherri Walker Vail, Dallas

Eric Westby, of Boston, wrote: "I recall reading in *Wired* a while
ago that people, presumably in Silicon Valley, were saying *triple-
dub*. I can't say it without feeling a little silly, though. I feel like I'm
trying to impress by being 'in the know.'" (Update: *triple-dub* has
never caught on.) John Davenport wrote: "I have been hearing
wuh-wuh-wuh. It is much easier to say than *dub-ya dub-ya dub-ya*
and does not sound nearly as pretentious as *triple-dub*." Jonathan
Gellman suggested *wow*, explaining: "This can be understood either as a universally accepted misspelling or as a synonym for
'world of (the) Web.' Jason Taniguchi, of Toronto, Ontario,
wrote: "My favourite response to this one is *wuhbuh buh*, which
trips nicely off the tongue, suggests threeness, and almost, if you
follow me, sounds like an anagram of 'w.'"

To me, the solution to this one seems obvious, except: should
we add those three "w"s together or multiply them, do you think?
Sextuple-u or *octuple-u*?

U

"We need a word to say to people who have just coughed. Coughing probably leads to death more often than sneezing does, but it is only sneezers who get wished good health (*gesundheit*) and blessed by God (*God bless you*). This is just not fair! Coughers deserve hearing comparable words or phrases of sympathy!"

—Richard Siegelman, East Norwich, N.Y.

This may be the hardest-to-relate-to word fugitive in the entire book. At least, when it was published in *The Atlantic*, only a small fraction of the usual number of responses came in. Olivia B. Snyder, of Philadelphia, wrote: "My grandmother always said (still does) *ooga booga*. Neither my mother nor I know why." Leo Schulte, of Toledo, Ohio, suggested, "Since Saint Blaise is the patron saint of throat ailments, how about *Blaise you!*" Nancy Ashmore, of Portsmouth, R.I., wrote: "I work with children, and here is what I say to coughers all the time: *Please cover your mouth*."

James Hilton, of Englewood, Colo., gave it his best shot. He wrote: "After someone coughs, you could say *geslungenaus*, meaning, 'Please stop—if you keep doing that, you're going to cough up your lungs.' You could say *gesbaggenheit*, meaning, 'Here, put this

131

bag over your head if you plan to keep doing that.' You could say *gessockenstuffen*, meaning, 'Keep that up and I'm going to have to gag you.' You could say *geskoffenmitschooten*, meaning, 'I'm sorry, but if you keep doing that, I'll put you out of your misery.' You could say *gesfatigenwheezin*, meaning . . ."

My favorite possibility came from Suzanne Ellison, of An-

TWELVE OF ONE, A DOZEN OF THE OTHER

Which dozen of the following words about words are from dictionaries, and which dozen aren't?

Antapology: a reply to an apology

Capoodle: to speak in a strange language when petting small animals

Eblandish: to get by coaxing or flattery

Eutrapely: pleasantness in conversation

Exonym: a name that foreigners use for a place

Gress: (rare) to stick to the point during a family argument

Kapula: in grammar, the reticulated participle, when juxtaposed transitively with a split infinitive

Kyriolexy: the use of literal expressions

Lexplexed: unable to find the correct spelling for a word in the dictionary because you don't know how to spell it

Licorice books: dark, twisted, and not to everyone's liking—but those who like them can't get enough

Nossob: any word that looks as if it's probably another word backward but turns out not to be

napolis, Md.—not that I expect to start hearing it on everyone's lips. Ellison wrote: "My Neapolitan grandfather had a 'blessing' to offer a cougher, and it has a nice touch of fatalism: *'Sper'e c'o purmone soje fatiche e ch' essa nun more.'* That bit of dialect translates, roughly, 'I hope you have some lung left and don't die.'"

Nymwit: someone who is always trying to make up clever words; also, someone who constantly makes up silly nicknames for people

Ollapod: a mixture of languages

Ollendorffian: written in the artificial and overly formal style of foreign-language phrase books

Paradiorthosis: a false correction

Pertainym: a name for an adjective that is usually defined with the phrase "of or pertaining to"

Raw-gabbit: speaking confidently on a subject of which one is ignorant

Sesquelingual: short of bilingual, said of a person who speaks one language well and "gets by" in a second

Stelliscript: that which is written in the stars

Tashivation: the art of answering without listening to questions

Traith: that which is lost in translation

Twone: a new name for portmanteau words: *two* words made into *one*

Ziraleet: an expression of joy

Zyxnoid: any word that a crossword puzzler makes up to complete the last blank

THE TWELVE AND THE DOZEN DISENTANGLED

The origins of our score plus four words about words.

Antapology, for a reply to an apology, appears in *Weird and Wonderful Words* and the *OED*.

Capoodle, for a way of speaking to small animals, was coined by Audrey Scholtmeijer, of Richmond, British Columbia; it appears in *Wanted Words 2*.

Eblandish, relating to coaxing or flattery, appears in *More Weird and Wonderful Words* and the *OED*. The word is both obsolete and rare; the *OED*'s lone citation is from 1623.

Eutrapely, for pleasantness in conversation, appears in *Weird and Wonderful Words* and the *OED*. According to *Weird and Wonderful*, it was "one of the seven moral virtues enumerated by Aristotle."

Exonym, a foreigners' name for a place, appears in *Weird and Wonderful Words* and online dictionaries. An example of an *exonym* is *Florence* for *Firenze*.

Gress, for sticking to the point, appears in *The Deeper Meaning of Liff*. Even so, it doesn't seem to be a place-name anywhere in the world.

Kapula, a pseudo-grammatical term, was coined for "A Volley of Words."

Kyriolexy, for the use of literal expressions, appears in *More Weird and Wonderful Words* and the *OED*.

Lexplexed, for that dictionary-related Catch-22, appears in *Unexplained Sniglets of the Universe*.

Licorice books was coined by Jean Matthews, according to her husband, Russ Lawrence, of Chapter One Book Store, in Hamilton, Mont. To clarify, Lawrence adds: "Think Chuck Palahniuk [the author of *Fight Club*] and his ilk."

Nossob is and means *not* spelled backward according to *The Deeper Meaning of Liff*. Elsewhere, it is a generally dry riverbed in south-central Africa.

Nymwit, a person who can't help making up clever words and silly nicknames, was coined by Charles Harrington Elster, of San Diego.

Ollapod, a mixture of languages, appears in *Xenia* and the *OED*. The word comes from the Spanish phrase *olla podrida*. Literally translated, this means "rotten pot," but for reasons that are "not known," according to the *OED*, it ordinarily refers to a spicy mixed Iberian stew.

Ollendorffian, "written in the . . . style of foreign-language phrase books," derives from the name of Heinrich Gottfried Ollendorff, a German educator who wrote foreign-language textbooks; it appears in *More Weird and Wonderful Words* and the *OED*. *More Weird and Wonderful* contains some hilarious examples of *Ollendorffian* English, including "Stop, the postilion has been struck by lightning!" and "Unhand me, Sir, for my husband, who is an Australian, awaits without."

Paradiorthosis, for a false correction, appears in *More Weird and Wonderful Words* and the *OED*.

Pertainym, for an adjective defined with the phrase "of or pertaining to," appears in *More Weird and Wonderful Words* and online dictionaries.

Raw-gabbit, for speaking confidently but ignorantly, appears in *A Scots Dialectic Dictionary* (1911), according to *The Word Museum*.

Sesquelingual, to refer to vaguely bilingual people, was coined by George Englebretsen, of Lennoxville, Quebec, as reported in *Family Words*.

Stelliscript, for what is written in the stars, appears in *A Supplemental English Glossary* (1881), according to *The Word Museum*.

Tashivation, for answering unthinkingly, was coined for *Burgess Unabridged*.

Traith, what is lost in translation, was coined by the writer Judith Kitchen, for *In a Word*.

Twone, as an updated name for portmanteau words, was coined by Glen Lee, of Monona, Wis., a reader of my Word Court newspaper column.

Ziraleet, for an expression of joy, appears in *Weird and Wonderful Words* and the *OED*.

Zyxnoid, a "word that a crossword puzzler makes up," appears in *Sniglets*. A near-synonym coined by the writer Mark J. Estren appears in *In a Word*: "*xltn*: The last four-letter word needed to complete a crossword puzzle." Estren notes: "Three-letter and five-letter variants of *xltn* have also been reported."

U

"Many of my friends, family, and acquaintances use the names of products as equivalent to their generic designations: *Kleenex* for 'facial tissues,' *Band-Aid* for 'bandage,' *Wite-Out* for 'typing-correction fluid,' *Xerox* for 'photocopy.' While I am convinced there is a word for this process of a trademark entering the vernacular, no one can tell me what it is. Without access to a reverse dictionary, I don't know if I'm totally off base here. Perhaps you can tell me."

—*Gregory Altreuter, New York City*

James Shull proposed: "*Trademark synecdoche?* Not terribly inventive or clever, but serviceable." Judy Lewis suggested *logodoption.* Michael Fischer wrote: "Why don't we try to make the word look like what it means: *xeroxidation? frigidarwinism? kleenextortion!* (By the way, would a person who coined such a word be called an *ycleptomaniac?*)"

Kristin Streck wrote: "There actually *is* a word for this. In business law they call it *generification* (of a trademark or brand name). In order to keep a copyright on the word, a company must prove generification has not occurred and/or that the company has taken reasonable steps to prevent it. This is why one sees ads that say things like 'You can't make a Xerox, but you can make the best-quality photocopy on a Xerox brand copier.' "

An Internet search, however, suggests that *generification* is little used in this sense. More often the word turns up in contexts like this: "The aim is to produce software that embodies functionality or characteristics that are common across the whole 'community.' We describe this as the principle of *generification*." Uh, OK. Recreational word coining this is not.

Maybe we should turn to a blogger named Colby Willen, of Birmingham, Ala., who introduced the coinage *logogenericism* on his blog about language in August 2004. Willen wrote, "Some people have tried the terms *eponym*, *generification*, and/or *metonymy* for this process, but none seem to quite fit." He defined *logogenericism* (which he has also entered into www.pseudodictionary.com) as "the evolution of a trademark name into a common name that transcends and is used to reference an entire product line." A little irony about this discussion of Willen's efforts: his blog appears on www.blogger.com (at vocabuli.blogspot.com), which is, of course, the non-logogeneric blogging site.

A different word, though, seems to be catching on. Coined by Paul McFedries on his Web site, The Word Spy, where it's defined as "a brand name that has become a generic name for its product category," the word is ***generonym.***

U

"There should be a good English word describing the realization of the perfect riposte three hours after the argument. The French use the term *esprit de l'escalier, n'est pas?* The Germans say *Treppenwitz*. We ought to have a word of our own."

—*Martin Borsanyi, Newport Beach, Calif.*

This question has never appeared in the Word Fugitives column, but the word is often sought, and many suggestions have been made. The earliest I know of comes from Gelett Burgess, who in *Burgess Unabridged* proposed *tintiddle*, "an imaginary conversation; wit coming too late." *In a Word* presents three possibilities: *hindser*, coined by the writer Nicholas Delbanco; *retrotort*, by the writer Bernard Cooper; and *stairwit*, by the writer Kirkpatrick Sale. Among all the coinages I've seen, though, my favorite comes from the writer James Alexander Thom, according to Ove Michaelsen in his unpublished manuscript *Verboddities*. Thom's word is **afterism.**

P.S.: Please see "Still at Large" at the end of this chapter for two related fugitives that have yet to be captured—by anyone, as far as I know.

U

"The word I'm looking for is a fugitive in an unusual sense, since there is an almost perfectly good English word for the concept already: *palindrome*, meaning, of course, 'a word or expression that reads the same forward and backward,' such as 'Madam, I'm Adam.' The only problem, as my son pointed out to me recently, is that *palindrome* is not itself a palindrome. It would be much nicer to have a word for this concept that was self-descriptive."

—*Max Hailperin, St. Peter, Minn.*

Robert Maier, of Southfield, Mich., has the solution to your problem—and solutions to several related problems as well. In an article originally published in *Word Ways: The Journal of Recreational Linguistics* in 1995, he wrote:

A concept as exquisite as palindromy deserves to have a name that is palindromic. In keeping with the spirit of the etymology, but adding the requirement of its being what it describes, we could do a lot worse than *palinilap*, from the Greek *palin* (again) and *nilap* (spelled backwards).

By adding the appropriate suffix to the back of the word and the reverse spelling of the suffix to its front, each of the parts of speech can be formed while still maintaining the word's self-reflecting quality. Thus the plural is *spalinilaps*, the adjectival form is *lapalinilapal*, the adverbial form is *yllapalinilapally* and the infinitive is *etapalinilapate*, which is conjugated as "I eta-palinilapate," "you etapalininlapate," "he/she/it setapalinilap-ates."

So there.

"Why is there no neutral word for the third-person singular pronoun? By neutral, I do not mean neuter. I am constantly annoyed at having to use *he or she* or the passive voice to refer to a 'generic' person. English experts have informed me that I can't correctly use *he, she, (s)he, they,* or *it*."

—*J. Kevin King, Tallahassee, Fla.*

Here Kevin King is innocently seeking the Holy Grail of word coining, recreational or otherwise. In a 1987 article in *The Washington Post*, John Algeo, then the editor of the Among the New Words column in the journal *American Speech*, explained, "Lots of people have tried to solve that problem. There have been chronicled some 60 such new pronouns." Algeo went on to explain that the gender-neutral pronoun that has come closest to being accepted into English is *thon*, which, he said, "was actually used for a while by *The Chicago Tribune* to replace *he* and *she*," and which appeared in *Webster's New International Dictionary*, second edition, unabridged. "*Webster's Second*" is copyright 1934; *thon* (said to be a contraction of *that one*) continued to turn up in printings of the dictionary until at least the mid-1950s.

But it never caught on. Even as *thon* sat waiting hopefully in *Webster's Second*, Albert H. Morehead, the editor of *The New American Dictionaries*, called the absence of such a pronoun one of the seven gaps in English that most desperately needed to be filled. Writing in *The New York Times Magazine* ("English at a Loss for Words") on September 11, 1955, Morehead said: "Nobody is likely to go as long as an hour without encountering this need. We have the plural *they* to apply to the genders indiscriminately: why must we be deprived of an equivalent singular word?"

Word coiners keep trying to fill this gap. In *In a Word*, the writer James Trefil proposes *gen* for this purpose; Professor Robin Fox proposes *sheeit*. Allan Metcalf, in his *Predicting New Words*, lists *shey*, *heshe*, *herm*, *em*, *en*, and *et* as some of the proposals that have been floated "over the centuries." He notes, however, that "English hasn't had a new pronoun for about a thousand years, and there is no sign it will acquire one any time soon."

SIX GRIZZLED FUGITIVES

❧❦

When, in 1955, the dictionary editor Albert H. Morehead (who was also the bridge [as in the card game] editor of *The New York Times*) declared a gender-neutral singular pronoun to be one of the words that English most needed, he listed it seventh, after six other fugitives. These were:

1. "A dignified word to replace the slang *boy friend*."
2. "A similar word for the woman in the case."
3. "One brief, acceptable word to mean *am not* in questions. . . . 'Aren't I?' is ungrammatical, 'Am I not?' has a stilted sound, and it has been deeply ingrained in our consciousness that 'Ain't I?' is vulgar and just plain wrong."
4. "A word that means either brother or sister, in the same way that *parent* means either father or mother."
5. "A word that means 'to state as an opinion.' The English word *opine* once expressed this meaning satisfactorily, but somehow in the last fifty years it has lost its respectability."
6. "A polite but noncommittal word that means simply 'I acknowledge having heard what you just said.' "

I wish Morehead were available to tell us whether *sibling* fills the bill for his word number 4, and if not, why not. All of his other words, though, are still absent from our language. Requests for most of them appear regularly in the Word Fugitives mailbag.

❧❦

RUSTLED UP

Paul Dickson, the author of numerous books on words (among other things), shared some words about words that he has coined over the years:

Demonym. A term that is used to describe a person from a particular geographic locale—for instance, *Hoosier* for a person from Indiana and *Liverpudlian* for a person from Liverpool. This coinage of mine was picked up and used by William Safire in his *New York Times* On Language column in late 1997. I just Googled *demonym* and got 7,350 hits.

Glenhaven. A name that is so innocuous or trite that you find it difficult to recall. Cedar Crest, Long Ridge, and Harbor View are all *glenhavens.*

Mxyzptlk. A person with a particularly difficult name to pronounce. Mxyzptlk is one of Superman's multitude of archenemies. An example of a *Mxyzptlkian* character was Joe Btfsplk, who used to appear in Al Capp's *Li'l Abner.*

Smirkword. A word or phrase that you can never again think of in the same light after learning of an earlier or alternative meaning. *Cleveland*, for instance, is a name that has had an entirely new ring to it since I discovered that it was once common slang for the female pudendum. Another example is *flux*, which can be a euphemism for diarrhea. The leading smirkword in contemporary speech is *nitty-gritty*. According to John Train in his *Remarkable Words*, this was, "originally, black slang for the inner end of vagina."

Word word. There are situations in which it is necessary to repeat a word in order to make sure someone knows what you are talking about. For instance, you might be asked "Are you talking about an American Indian or an Indian Indian?" Or "Oh, you're talking about grass grass. I thought you were talking about grass."

William A. Sabin, the author of *The Gregg Reference Manual*, wrote me:

Cushaw. Many years ago, at dinner with my wife and five children, my ten-year-old son John asked me the meaning of *cushaw*. My experience as a father had taught me that children crave certainty more than they crave truth, so I looked John in the eye and in my most authoritative voice told him a cushaw was a form of yellow squash. Since I had already acquired a reputation for making up answers, John said he didn't believe me. Brazening it out, I encouraged him to go to a dictionary. Which he did. John came running back a minute later with his eyes bugging out, and he reported that a cushaw was indeed a kind of squash. Now I, with *my* eyes bugging out, ran to the dictionary to discover that I had indeed hit on the right definition.

Since that time, *cushaw* in our family lexicon has come to stand for any answer made up on the spot to satisfy someone else's urgent need to know. The fact that the answer might coincidentally turn out to be true is not really material.

There is a postscript to this story. A few years ago, John (now in his early forties) cornered me one evening when we were alone and feeling a little mellow. John said: "Remember years ago when I asked you what a cushaw was and you made up an answer and then you were so shocked to discover that the answer was actually true? You really knew all along what a cushaw was, didn't you?" After I stopped laughing, I asked John what had made him suspect me after all these years. He explained that he'd been browsing in a used-book store and wound up in the section that had old cookbooks. As he went through the section on vegetables, he found a recipe for cooking cushaws, and then it hit him: "My father has always liked to look at old cookbooks. That's why he would know what a cushaw is."

If there is a moral to this story, it's that a successful creator of cushaws will keep his listeners in doubt as to whether or not the answer to the question is true. Years later, at a small dinner party with people we did not know, I was asked the origin of the initials *OK*. When I referred to Martin Van Buren and Old Kinderhook, my wife guffawed and said, "Listen to that man. Did you ever know anyone who could make up crazy explanations like that on the spur of the moment?" When our host returned with a dictionary that vindicated me, I was able to enjoy a brief and all-too-infrequent sense of victory over my much more knowledgeable wife.

Faith Eckler, whose husband is the editor of *Word Ways: The Journal of Recreational Linguistics*, wrote me:

From time immemorial our family has deliberately mispronounced words. An example of this is the word *agenda*, where we always emphasize the first syllable and use a hard "g." We use this word often, as in "What's today's *agenda*?" In other words, What's the plan for today?

We also like to create similar-sounding but humorous names for businesses and institutions. We buy our groceries at *Ship Rot* (Shop Rite) or the *Big Onion* (Grand Union). We read our newspaper *The Daily Wretched* (*The Daily Record*), and I volunteer at a local nursing home, *Morbid View* (Morris View). Our daughter graduated from *Fairly Ridiculous* (Fairleigh Dickinson) University.

We deliberately transpose syllables. We sometimes go to *Merhiker* (Herkimer), which is adjacent to *I Lion* (Ilion). We attend the *Episcolopian* Church, and thereby hangs a tale.

My family always said that we were *Episcolopians*, and I mistakenly thought that was simply a case of putting the em*phas*is on the wrong syl*lab*le. When filling out my application to Swarthmore College, I carefully spelled out *Episcolopian* where it asked for religion. At the very last moment I realized my mistake and had to erase the offending word—no mean task when applications were filled out in pen and ink. It left not only a smudge but a small hole in the paper. Nonetheless, Swarthmore accepted me.

And Dave Morice, the editor of the Kickshaws column in *Word Ways*, sent me this work in progress:

XICTIONARY: A Dictionary of Words Beginning With "X"

"X" is the least-used letter in English. It is made in one of the most basic ways possible—two lines crossing each other. This suggests that "X" should be one of the most-used letters. *Xictionary* provides many new X-words to help "X" catch up with the twenty-five other letters. Here are twenty-six X-words and their definitions. I plan on adding twenty-six entries for each X-plus-other-letter combo. XB——, XC——, etc., for a total of $26 \times 26 = 676$ entries in the *Xictionary*.

> *Xaariot*: a whisk broom on a desert island
> *Xabtunkle*: the hard skeleton secreted by a raindrop prior to a storm
> *Xacon*: a religious sect that moves on or as if on a seesaw
> *Xadpipzip*: to eat bits of cowhide during a rodeo
> *Xaeulio*: a lively dance by a dull person
> *Xaffxiff*: to crumple a small animal
> *Xaggyplaggy*: a hairstyle that combines the worst attributes of mullets and dreadlocks
> *Xahaha*: the act or sound of laughing at an odor left in passing

Xaitcch: derived from or depending upon a beautiful, dangerous woman

Xajpimmery: a towel for drying a man's wig

Xakknaw: a loose gown worn in bed by the female deity Fascinakka in ancient Micronesian mythology

Xallo: a game of discards

Xaminthooboiboi: to pound one's fist on a melon

Xankzchpt: a scratch on a brand-new car

Xao: an extremely cruel form of Zen practiced by malcontents at airports

Xapxapxap: very, very, very, very, very sharp

Xaque: sensiblenessless

Xargruoalf: the sound of wind blowing over a house of cards

Xastically: in a crude or viscous [*sic*] manner

Xatzaroouu: the surtax on bikinis

Xauglate: to make the throaty cry of an angry, extinct carnivore late at night

Xavleentnary: not drunk, but not sober

Xawatdi: a chestnut or chestnuts roasting on a Class C fire

Xax: slang term for abominably bad taste in footwear

Xaybot: a robot gone out of control in a world populated by androids

Xazzik: a type of jacknail used with a left-handed jackhammer

STILL AT LARGE

Evidently, our language has neglected itself: it has no words to describe many kinds of familiar words and phrases. Let's help English out and come up with some of these.

"What would be a term for someone whose first and last names are names that could be first names, like John Lester or James Thomas?"

—*Richard Kreibich, Milton, Wis.*

"Is there a term for those business names (like Hair Apparent, Shear Madness, Sofa So Good, Consign Mint, and my all-time favorite, One if by Bagel) with a pun or wordplay in them? And why are so many of them hair salons?"

—*Kevin Read, New York City*

"Sometimes when a single word is repeated and I'm closely examining the writing, I find myself at a point of overexposure—and suddenly the word seems wrong. Alien. Strange, as if in some foreign language. The word seems to beg, 'How did we ever decide that this combination of sounds should have this meaning?' I remember it happening with the word *purse*, and just recently with *first*. Oddly enough, it's the simplest words that seem to elicit this response. And we still don't know what to call it."

—*Jim Harrison, Gainesville, Fla.*

"My father has wondered for years if there is a word for the practice of answering a question with a question. One linguist I queried said that it is not possible to *answer* a question with a question. So I suppose I should rephrase and ask if there is a word that describes the act of responding to a question with a question."

—*E. C. White, Poway, Calif.*

"I'm looking for a term for when people ask and answer their own questions in a yes-and-no format. It seems to be getting very common. For example, someone might say: 'Were some mistakes made? Yes. Can we improve? Yes. Were we negligent in our duties? No.'"

—*Chris King, Rochester, N.Y.*

"I am looking for a word to describe the deliberate misspelling of words and phrases for marketing purposes. For example, *Citibank*, *Rite Aid*, *Kool-Aid*, and *Krispy Kreme*. It drives me crazy!"

—*Melissa Harris, Brooklyn, N.Y.*

"What might we call famous expressions that purportedly are quotations from well-known sources but are the result of invention or inexact recall—for instance, 'Play it again, Sam' and 'Elementary, my dear Watson'?"

—*Patrick Ivers, Laramie, Wyo.*

"Is there a word for something that sounds like a euphemism but isn't? For instance, the other day I was salting cucumbers for a Middle Eastern salad I like to make. Guests were present, so I said, 'Excuse me, I have to go turn over my cucumbers.' You should have seen the expressions on their faces."

—*Willa Bluebird, Bumpas, Va.*

"My question is about acronyms and initialisms. NASA, for instance, is quite an efficient acronym, using two spoken syllables to replace fourteen (*National Aeronautics and Space Administration*). But I am looking for a word for an 'abbreviation' that is longer than the phrase it replaces. My favorite example is *www*, which at nine syllables is exactly three times as long as the phrase it replaces: *World Wide Web*."

—*Wes Jones, Wilmington, Del.*

"I work in the insurance industry, and today a colleague plaintively asked: Is there an acronym to describe an organization overrun with acronyms?"

—*Kirsten Finlayson, Pittsburgh, Pa.*

"Is there a word for when someone 'says' an action instead of performing it? For instance, when someone, upon entering a room, says 'knock knock,' instead of actually knocking. Or when someone, as a greeting or good-bye, says 'kiss kiss' instead of actually giving the person a kiss on either cheek? Whatever the word is, it should contain a hint of how annoying this quirk is."

—*Hunter Slaton, Brooklyn, N.Y.*

"Is there a term for those metaphorical insults like 'She's one sandwich short of a picnic' and 'He's not the sharpest knife in the drawer'?"

—*Joel Blum, San Francisco*

"Of course, *l'esprit de l'escalier* and *Treppenwitz* are terms that exist to describe the perfect witty phrase or comeback that comes to you after the appropriate moment has passed. I'm looking for a term to describe this phenomenon when the perfect but too-late rejoinder occurs not to you but to a third party."

—*Collenette Scott, Toronto, Ontario*

"The French have a colorful expression: *l'esprit de l'escalier*. I'd like a word that describes the next step, where in subsequent retellings the imagined version becomes the 'true' version—or even the *next* step, where the narrator tells the revised version so many times as to become convinced that the imagined version is what was actually said.

"I was reminded of this question last night when I was telling some colleagues a story: As counsel to a small African nation, I dropped off an item at an adversary's hotel (he was counsel for another African nation). While waiting for him to appear, I had a drink at the bar. In the telling, I always charge the drink to the adversary's room—but I no longer remember whether I actually dared, or merely thought about it."

—Lorraine Charlton, Guilford, Conn.

ODDS AND ENDS

Nouns, verbs, and a sprinkling of adjectives: these make up nearly all the word fugitives on our culture's "Wanted" list. Years ago, on the "Word Fugitives" Web page, I posted a request for a one-word preposition that would mean "in spite of or perhaps because of." You'd be surprised how often that wordy locution comes up. But, nobody bit, as I recall, and now that Web page itself has gone missing.

As for which nouns, verbs, and adjectives people most often or most avidly want—well, by now you've seen nearly the full gamut for yourself. I might have expected to get more fugitives relating to the cute things that children do. Similarly, the cute things pets do. And physical sensations. And things spiritual and metaphysical. And altered states—for instance, particular types of drunkenness, not-quite-hallucinations, having just won the lottery, going limp from an excess of laughing, and the mental composure required to react decently when other people manifest any of the foregoing. But we'll have to wait for another day to explore these subjects in any depth.

What remains for us to do now is investigate a few final, miscellaneous fugitives. This chapter is where the word fugitives go if they don't fit into any of the other categories—just so we're clear about what the organizing principle is here.

"What is a word to describe someone who, in looking up a word in the dictionary, is compelled to look across the page for another, equally interesting entry?"

—*John F. Schilke, Oregon City, Ore.*

In their responses to this question, people often came up with analogies or metaphors—for instance, *Webster surfer*. Trish Anderton, of Berlin, N.H., suggested *word-dogging* for the activity and used her coinage in a sentence: "Like a setter intent on sniffing out prey, she went *word-dogging* across the page." Ed Masten, of Memphis, Tenn., wrote, "My own word search is often distracted by *afliteration*, like a bee in a bed of begonias." William R. Phillips, of Seattle, wrote, more ominously, "Some fear that excessive use of the dictionary leads to *refer madness* and is a gateway to stronger language."

Travel-related metaphors are especially popular. Louis Greenwald, of Sacramento, wrote: "I have been doing that for years. I like to think of myself as a *word traveler*." Rob Longley, of Delmar, N.Y., wrote, "I think of myself as a *speechcomber*." Larry Malcus, of San Leandro, Calif., wrote, "I am afflicted with *wanderlex*." Steven L. Auslander, of Tucson, Ariz., wrote: "If someone consulting the dictionary is doing so in order to add words to a spoken diatribe, he or she may be described as a *hunter-blatherer*. If, instead, he is genuinely interested in the other words on the page, he may be called a *lexplorer*."

Daniel J. Scheub, of Dixon, Ill., suggested *rubricnecker*. David Terrell, of St. Louis, submitted *addictionado*, on behalf of the tenth-grade English class he teaches. Sara Stadler Nelson, of Atlanta, wrote: "My mother grew up in a tiny town in central Nebraska, and she entertained herself with the dictionary in precisely this way. She went on to earn a perfect score on the Test of Standard Written English. She was, of course, an *autodidict*."

Josh Simons, of Sharon, Mass., suggested, "Perhaps this is an example of *double-entry lookkeeping*." That's fun. But the term that Steven Clemens, of Maplewood, Mo., came up with is even more fun (and don't forget that we wanted a word for the person, not the activity): ***double-entry bookpeeker***.

U

"What do you call it when an individual nods off for a few seconds and then jolts awake? I have observed this and also been a victim, falling asleep in a public situation only to draw attention to myself as I snap out of it as if in the electric chair. Any suggestions?"

—Michael Murphy, Vancouver, British Columbia

If this letter makes you worry about the guy who wrote it, you're not alone. "Nodding out and snapping back to life is the core experience of an opiate high," warned Richard Kleiner, of Las Vegas, in a scary-looking memo sent from Intervention Headquarters at Arbitronix, where Kleiner works. Max Uhler, of Minneapolis, wrote, "This behavior is commonly seen among the gravely sick." "Tell him to see his doctor," urged Verba Weaver, of Lake Elmo, Minn. Addressing the letter's author directly, Laszlo Javorik, of Oregon, Ill., wrote: "Be careful!!! Especially if the symptoms appear together with extraordinary thirst, you may be diabetic! Get your blood sugar and your glucohemoglobin tested immediately!!!"

Many other people suggested medical terms that might apply. We asked John Shepard, the medical director of the Sleep Disorders Center at the Mayo Clinic, in Rochester, Minn., to choose among them, and he responded that *hypnic jerk* seemed to best fit the symptoms described. (He also reassured us that the great majority of people who experience hypnic jerks have nothing to worry about.) But of course that's medical jargon; we were looking for something more entertaining. Martin St-André, of Montreal, Quebec, shared a local idiom: "The expression we have is *cogner des clous*, more or less translatable as 'hammering nails' or maybe 'pounding nails with one's head.'" Kim Jastremski, of Murray, Ky., wrote: "One of my favorite phrases in Polish describes just this kind of sleep. The Poles say *to sleep like a woodpecker.*"

Other possibilities include *cornpecking* (Stu Thompson, of Littleton, Colo.), *napoplexy* (Merri Johnson, of Auburn, Neb.), *snaptime* (Roger Barkan, of Berkeley Heights, N.J.), *dozedive* (Cindie Farley, of Pacific Grove, Calif.), *the bobs* (Roy W. McLeese III, of Washington, D.C.), *nodding off and on* (Seth Eisner, of Arlington Heights, Ill.), *a wake-up fall* (Liz Bennett Bailey, of Doylestown, Pa.), and *kitnap* (Ben Grossblatt and Sara Debell, of Seattle).

We're getting there. Wayne Otto, of Middleton, Wis., wasn't the only person to suggest his word, but he made the case for it both early and persuasively. "If a short, refreshing snooze is a *catnap*," he wrote, "then a short but abruptly terminated snooze must be a ***catsnap***."

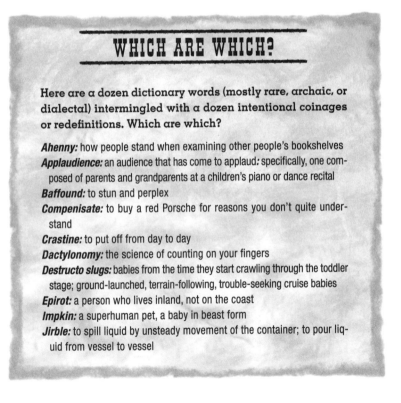

U

"Thin women: 'petite,' 'athletic,' 'slender.' Larger women: 'buxom,' 'full-figured,' 'Rubenesque.' Women in between?

WHICH ARE WHICH?

Here are a dozen dictionary words (mostly rare, archaic, or dialectal) intermingled with a dozen intentional coinages or redefinitions. Which are which?

Ahenny: how people stand when examining other people's bookshelves

Applaudience: an audience that has come to applaud: specifically, one composed of parents and grandparents at a children's piano or dance recital

Baffound: to stun and perplex

Compenisate: to buy a red Porsche for reasons you don't quite understand

Crastine: to put off from day to day

Dactylonomy: the science of counting on your fingers

Destructo slugs: babies from the time they start crawling through the toddler stage; ground-launched, terrain-following, trouble-seeking cruise babies

Epirot: a person who lives inland, not on the coast

Impkin: a superhuman pet, a baby in beast form

Jirble: to spill liquid by unsteady movement of the container; to pour liquid from vessel to vessel

'Medium.' Not even dress shops have a flattering word for women who are just right. Please help me before I seek such a woman in a personal ad."

—*Roger Wilson, Roanoke, Va.*

Merry-go-sorry: a mixture of laughing and crying

Mocteroof: the craft of dressing up damaged fruits and vegetables, practiced by produce sellers

Nudiustertian: of the day before yesterday

Origasmi: the Japanese art of folding paper marital aids

Paneity: the quality, fact, or state of being bread

Pang-wangle: a cheeriness under minor discomforts, a humorous optimism under small misfortunes

Penultimatum: "I'm going to tell you this only one more time after this . . ."

PIYAN: (acronym for "Plus If You Act Now"): any miscellaneous item thrown in on a late-night television ad

Pugnozzle: to move the nostrils and upper lip in the manner of a pug dog

Quatressential: not quite quintessential

Ruly: obedient

Toemostat: the foot or part of it that is extended from beneath the covers to control body temperature at night

Upstale: formerly fashionable among the beautiful people

Zumbooruk: a small swivel-gun, especially one mounted on the back of a camel

WHICH *ARE* WHICH

The dictionary words and the coinages explained.

Ahenny is the way people stand when examining other people's book-shelves, according to *The Deeper Meaning of Liff*. Otherwise, it's a village in Tipperary, Ireland, known for its ancient monastery.

Applaudience, an audience that has come to applaud, was coined by a listener to WRC radio, Washington, D.C., and appears in *Family Words*.

Baffound, to stun and perplex, is a dictionary word. It appears in *A Glossary of Mid-Yorkshire* (1876), according to *The Word Museum*.

Compenisate, to buy a red Porsche for reasons unknown, was coined by Stephen Dudzik, of Olney, Md., for The Style Invitational.

Crastine, to put off from day to day, appears in *An English Dictionary* (1713), according to *The Word Museum*.

Dactylonomy, meaning "counting on your fingers," is a dictionary word. It appears in *More Weird and Wonderful Words* and—along with other *dactylo-* words, including *dactylogram*, "a fingerprint"—in the *Oxford English Dictionary*.

Destructo slugs, meaning "terrain-following, trouble-seeking cruise babies," was coined by Shawn Fitzpatrick, of Johnson City, N.Y., and was heard on *All Things Considered* in July of 1995.

Epirot, a person who lives inland, appears in *More Weird and Wonderful Words* and the *OED*. A modern non-dictionary word with a similar meaning is *flyover people*.

Impkin, a baby in beast form, was coined for *Burgess Unabridged*.

Jirble, to spill or pour liquid, is a dictionary word. It appears in *More Weird and Wonderful Words*, which says it is "of onomatopoeic origin."

Merry-go-sorry, a mixture of laughing and crying, is a dictionary word, appearing in *The Encyclopaedic Dictionary* (1894), according to *The Word Museum*.

Mocteroof, dressing up damaged fruits and vegetables, is a mid-1800s dictionary word "of obscure origin," according to *Forgotten English*.

Nudiustertian, of the day before yesterday, appears in *More Weird and*

Wonderful Words and the *OED*. It comes from a Latin phrase whose literal meaning is "today the third day."

Origasmi, the art of folding paper marital aids, was coined by Philip M. Cohen, of Washington, D.C., for The Style Invitational.

Paneity, meaning "being bread," appears in *There's a Word for It* and the *OED*.

Pang-wangle, a cheeriness under minor discomforts, appears in the 1908 magazine article "Improvised Words."

Penultimatum, "I'm going to tell you this only one more time after this . . . ," was coined by Dot Yufer, of Newton, W.Va., for The Style Invitational.

PIYAN, standing for "Plus If You Act Now," appears in *Sniglets*.

Pugnozzle, to move the nostrils and upper lip in the manner of a pug dog, appears in *More Weird and Wonderful Words* and the *OED*. Samuel Beckett used the word in his 1934 short-story collection *More Pricks Than Kicks*.

Quatressential, meaning "not quite quintessential," was coined for "A Volley of Words."

Ruly, obedient, appears in *The Word Museum* and the *OED*. It was originally (circa 1400) derived from *rule* + *y*. People who use it nowadays, though, tend to think of it as a humorous back-formation from *unruly*.

Toemostat, for what's extended from beneath the covers to control body temperature, was coined by Arlene Zsilka, of Redford, Mich., a reader of my Word Court newspaper column.

Upstale, formerly fashionable, was coined for *Not the Webster's Dictionary*, which is indeed not a dictionary.

Zumbooruk, a camel-mounted swivel-gun, appears in the *OED*. It is derived from a Persian word for "hornet."

This request elicited a bit of feminist commentary. Denise Mathew, of Charlottesville, Va., wrote: "I was sad to see that you printed Roger Wilson's awful query. Please tell him to try using the word *Barbie*." Most women who responded, however, took no offense. For instance, Anne Quigg, of Malden, Mass. wrote, "My entry is *Our Bodies, Our 12s*." And Sharon Urquhart, of Graton, Calif., wrote: "The woman he seeks is a *femme mid-all*. Thanks for amusing me!"

The most popular coinages, submitted by members of both sexes, were *belle-curved* and *mediyum* or *mediyummy*. And here's a nice try that, alas, probably wouldn't get the point across: Jim Richards, of Rexburg, Idaho, suggested *nonplussed*.

But it is impossible to deny David Olivett, of Emporium, Pa., top honors. He sent in a poem, explaining, "I could not think of a one-word adjective to aid Roger Wilson in his plight. However, he is free to use this bit of doggerel: *'While the violin is small and sleek, / And the double bass broad and mellow, / The one true love that I do seek / Should mostly resemble a cello.'* "

U

Ralph W. Milligan, of Lake Charles, La.; Marion Greenman, of Oak Park, Ill.; and Jack Wilson, of Wayland, Mass., all separately sought one particular word—a pretty good hint that the lack of it is widely felt. As Milligan explained the word

fugitive in question, "The English language desperately needs a word for an offspring who is an adult. My eldest daughter is still my daughter, but she is certainly no longer my child."

Michael Fischer, of Minneapolis, responded with a list: "For the pedantic, there are *progeny* and *scions*; for insurance purposes, there is *descendants*; and if you want to be biblical, there is *begats*." Carolyn Roosevelt, of Cambridge, Mass., reported, more flippantly, "My cousin calls her grown progeny *my adults*." And Dan Dillon, of Chicago, thought to coin *unchildren*.

Charles Harrington Elster, of San Diego, however, coined what sounds to me like the perfect term. "Assuming the child has left home," he wrote, "how about *offsprung*?"

"I'd like a verb meaning 'to go to do something and return having absentmindedly done one or more other things instead.'"

—*Jonathan Zuber, Winston-Salem, N.C.*

Matt Mayberry, of Colorado Springs, Colo., had no verb to suggest—but he acutely feels the need for one. He wrote: "My colleagues and I were discussing just this tendency. I work in a history museum surrounded by a wide variety of fascinating artifacts, documents, problems, and projects. We often set out from our work areas determined to accomplish one thing, only to return some significant time later having taken a circuitous route through the building. When we do return to our desks, not only is our original task unfulfilled, but we often can't recall why we left in the first place."

Mike Olesak, of Perth Amboy, N.J., wrote: "I just saw a comic of Beetle Bailey in which General Halftrack gets sidetracked when he leaves the kitchen to go get the paper and returns, nine distracted frames later, with a flyswatter. I've experienced this phenomenon myself. It seems as though the mind gets spaced out on tangents; for a split second you seem to be in another world. So my submission would be *nether-minded*."

Task turns up in many coinages intended to meet this need. For instance, Jim Tanner, of Fort Collins, Colo., suggested that the "much-achieved if not much-sought-after capability" in question might be called *muddletitasking*. Or it might be *alti-tasking* (Sam Putnam, of Vallejo, Calif.), *faulty-tasking* (Janet Watson, of Norwell, Mass.), or *mistask* (lots of people).

But here's an original word that gets straight to the point: **onthewaylaid** (Marshall Arbitman, of New York City).

ACCURATELY QUOTED

The Washington Post's Style Invitational contest invited readers to "take any word, put a portion of it in 'air quotes' and redefine the word." For example, Jean Sorensen, of Herndon, Va., sent in *"Gall"*o: "the nerve to bring cheap wine." In each of the following words, where do the air quotes go?

Abutting: dancing cheek to cheek
Cluelessness: a tendency to miss the point entirely
Conversion: "Glory hallelujah, I have found God, now let me out of jail."
Elite: people who become rich or powerful not through ability but rather through inheritance
Fabrication: a rave movie review written by someone who doesn't exist
Figurine: one of those novelty garden fountains
Fungicide: a killjoy
Gangster: someone torn by inner conflict, and bullets
Psychopath: Lizzie Borden
Septuagenarian: an old man who chews tobacco
Slaughter: "Stop! You're killing me!"
Terrapin: the person holding up the line at the ATM because he cannot recall his number

ACCURATELY QUOTED AND MARKED

One kind of dancing cheek to cheek is *a"butt"ing* (Bill Strider, of Gaithersburg, Md.).

The tendency to miss the point entirely is *"cluelessness"* (Jacob Weinstein, of Los Angeles).

"Glory hallelujah, I have found God, now let me out of jail" would be a *"con"version* (Gary Mason, of Herndon, Va.).

People who become rich or powerful not through ability but rather through inheritance are the *e"lite"* (Art Grinath, of Takoma Park, Md.).

A rave movie review written by someone who doesn't exist is a *"fab"rication* (Jennifer Hart, of Arlington, Va.).

That novelty garden fountain is a *fig"urine"* (T. J. Murphy, of Arlington, Va.; Frank Thomson, of Largo, Fla.).

A killjoy is *"fun"gicide* (Dave Ferry, of Leesburg, Va.).

Someone torn by inner conflict, and bullets, is a *g"angst"er* (Tom Witte, of Montgomery Village, Md.).

Lizzie Borden was a *psy"chop"ath* (Noah Kady, of Myersville, Md.; Merrill Bates Jr., of Severna Park, Md.).

An old man who chews tobacco is a *se"ptua"genarian* (Dudley Thompson, of Derwood, Md.).

"Stop! You're killing me!" yields *s"laughter"* (Elden Carnahan, of Laurel, Md.).

The person holding up the ATM line because he cannot recall his number is a *terra"pin"* (Jennifer Hart, of Arlington, Va.).

U

"The Russian father-in-law of my recently married son asked me what the English word is to describe our new relationship to each other as parents of the bride and groom. He offered the Russian word *svaty*, since there doesn't seem to be an English word."

—*Barbara Kelly, Palo Alto, Calif.*

Over the centuries English has assimilated words from dozens of languages, a number of which do have words for this relationship—Yiddish, for instance. Herb Zweig, of Woodland Hills, Calif., wrote: "See Leo Rosten's *The Joys of Yiddish*. *Machetayneste* (the *ch* is guttural) means the mother of your child's spouse; *machuten* means the father of your child's spouse; and *machetunim* means the extended family of your spouse, so it describes these relationships from the children's point of view. Rosten tells an old joke: Why did Adam and Eve live so long? Because they had no *machetunim*."

Other people invoke other languages. Sally Sordinas, of Corfu, Greece, wrote, "My Greek son-in-law's mother calls me *symbethèra*." Roberta Kedzierski, of Milan, Italy, wrote, "There is a word in Italian: *consuoceri*." Several people wrote to say that in Spanish the term is *consuegros*. Note, however, the masculine *o* preceding the plural *s*. Barry Hammel, of Santa Ana, Costa Rica, warned: "In these days of gender sensibility, using just the male term for both (as in Spanish) is a no-no. Even in Spanish one occasionally sees written, among the e-mail crowd, such things as *compañer@s* to replace *compañeros y compañeras*."

Dan Moerman, a professor of anthropology at the University of Michigan at Dearborn, submitted a veritable treatise about terminology used in his profession, including the following: "*Consanguineal*, or blood, relatives are all those people with whom you share an ancestor. *Affinal* relatives, or in-laws, are all your relatives by marriage. For the parents of the bride and groom, *affines* is a perfectly acceptable term."

And Ernie Joaquin, of DeKalb, Ill., wrote: "In the Philippines the Tagalog term for the relationship between parents of bride and groom is **magbalae**. They call one another, or they are called, **balae**." Admittedly, no more than any of the other suggestions do these terms seem poised to enter the American English mainstream. But Tagalog is so intriguingly exotic. From the folks who brought us *ylang-ylang* and *boondocks*, then, shall we borrow **balae**?

U

"Is there an antonym for *synergy*?"
            —*Gerald Brown, Pebble Beach, Calif.*

Thomas Ferrell, of Miami, reported, "My dictionary gives *antienergistic* as an antonym for *synergistic*, in the sense of yielding to energy applied from without." *Chaos, cosinergy,* and *syntropy* are other physics-major-type words that were proposed.

Emily Scott, of Newton, Mass., wrote: "My dictionary defines *synergy* as 'combined or cooperative action or force,' and so in my quest for an antonym, *divorce* came quickly to mind." Brooks Fudenberg, of San Francisco, wrote: "Too easy! The antonym for *synergy* must be *saintgy*." People whose minds tend in yet other directions offered up such suggestions as *government, bureaucracy,* and *Congress.*

For once, though, perhaps there's no better answer to this question than another question. (By the way, a word for answering a question with a question is a fugitive still at large—please see the end of Chapter Five.) Bhagwan Chowdhry, of Los Angeles, wrote, **"Is looking for an antonym for *synergy* equivalent to looking for a synonym for *antergy*?"**

"As a soccer coach for kindergartners, I encourage the kids to become comfortable controlling the ball with either foot. There's a word for this with the hands: *ambidextrous.* Surely there should be one for the feet. I've used *ambifooterous,* as

ambipederous sounds awkward. It always gets a laugh, but is there a proper word for this?"

—*Vicki Yuen, Las Vegas*

A person looking for a "proper" word has probably come to the wrong place, but let's give it a go. John Siddeek, of Grand Junction, Colo., responded: "I, too, am a soccer coach, and each season I give an award to the player who is the best at using both feet. I have titled this at various times the Ambipedal Award, the Bipedal Award, the Amphibian Award, and the Ambipedarocious Award." Siddeek went on to make a point also made by a number of other people. For instance, Philip L. Salgado, of Spokane, Wash., wrote: "The word *ambidextrous* makes no reference to the hand: *ambi-* 'both,' *dexter* 'right.' Could not *ambidextrous* be used by a soccer coach to describe the desired skill and perhaps teach a little language as well?"

People had fun coining the likes of *switch kickers*, *bipedept*, *omnbootsman*, *bilegual*, and *gambidextrous*. But as it turned out, a less inventive approach achieved the goal brilliantly. "There is in fact a very simple term that is used by all coaches, players, and fans in the UK," wrote Allan Sutherland, of Aberdeen, Scotland. "It is *two-footed*, as in 'He's a *two-footed* player,' which is not so much stating the obvious as describing the ability to use either foot equally well. Though I can think of no other pastime except perhaps flirting under restaurant tables which can benefit from this skill, I would like both to inform you that the term is standard in football and to suggest that it might be used for all foot activities."

RUSTLED UP

The poet and Pulitzer Prize–winning music critic Lloyd Schwartz wrote me:

My favorite "personal" word is *snoozle*, which means a nap taken (noun), or to take a nap (verb), with someone one is especially fond of. I suppose this could include a child taking a nap with a parent, but I imagine it mainly suggesting a nap as a romantic prelude, interlude, or postlude. Definitely *ludic* on some level.

P.S.: A friend of mind, the artist Ralph Hamilton, imagines a luxury make-out limo called the *Cuddillac*, which would be the perfect vehicle in which one could *snoozle*.

Thierry Fontenelle, a computational linguist in the Microsoft Speech and Natural Language Group, wrote me:

Recently I took a few days off with my family on the San Juan Islands, between Seattle and Canada. While I was on these islands, I realized that there was no McDonald's, no Kentucky Fried Chicken or any other fast-food restaurant there. The food we ate was mainly organic, and I realized there were plenty of inhabitants and visitors who only opted for bio products. This also made me realize that a word like *biotarian* is perhaps needed in the English lexicon. *Vegetarian* is much too restrictive, since *biotarians* also eat bio chicken and various types of bio meat, for instance.

Note that I very much prefer *biotarian*, coined like *vegetarian*, to *biovore* (*omnivore*), given all the connotations that surround the former term. Environmentally friendly people are more likely to be *biotarians*, I guess.

James Trager, the author of the popular *Chronologies* books, wrote me:

Walt Disney gave the hands of Mickey Mouse and his other characters only four fingers; he saved tons of money in animation costs in those days before computers. In more modern times, we have *burbs*, *hoods*, *copters*, and *zines*. It bugs my granddaughters when they hear me talking about *mercials*, *ditioners*, and *puters*. They raise their eyebrows when I say I'm *zausted*. But when they're older, they'll realize that these truncated neologisms are harmless compared with the late Joe McCarthy's use of *Democrat* as an adjective, a practice still followed by right-wing extremists. Lately I've been using the term *servatives* for those folks who call themselves conservatives but seem bent on serving various special interests rather than the general good.

STILL AT LARGE

 A few nonexistent oddities and entities, for your pleasure.

"A female equivalent of *virility*. *Lustiness* will not do. *Lust* is defined in *Webster's* as 'vehement or longing affection or de-

sire,' and its root is Old English 'pleasure.' *Virile* has as part of its definition in *Webster's* 'sturdy, intrepid, and forceful,' equated with 'having the characteristics of manhood.' In common usage it is also applied to sexual performance as a compliment, a positive trait. I can't think of one stand-alone epithet that conveys the same meaning for women and has positive, powerful connotations. We need a word that conveys female sexual prowess, ability to bear children, and general womanly vigor and love of pleasure. To me, *virile* bears all of those connotations for a man."

—*Maighread Medbh, Swords, County Dublin, Ireland*

"Is there a word for almost needing a haircut but not quite?"

—*Doris Fleischman, Albany, N.Y.*

"What about the thing a dog does when it goes around and around and around before it lies down? What is it doing?"

—*Anne Bernays, Cambridge, Mass.*

"As a world-class procrastinator, I am, instead of writing an overdue seminar paper, making a request for a word for those piddling chores that suddenly become unusually pressing or fascinating once one has a more objectively important and grueling task at hand. There should be a word for the things that I spend roughly half of my waking hours doing, in order to avoid my real work. When else, after all, will the toilet get cleaned, the junk drawer de-junked, and the paper clips all turned in the same direction?"

—*Jenny Sakai, New York City*

"There ought to be a word, parallel to 'gossiping,' for having social conversations about technological things: comparing kinds of new televisions or the merits of different digital cameras or cell phones."

—*Hatsy Shields, Hamilton, Mass.*

"I find it quite astonishing that in English there is no word for the sound produced by a camel. As you know, the camel is the most important animal in the Muslim world. In the midst of so much talk about the clash of civilizations, wouldn't coining such a word help, albeit in a small way, to create a discourse?"

—*M. A. Moftah, Cairo, Egypt*

IN CONCLUSION: KEEPERS

Just about any syllable or series of syllables *could* mean just about anything in English. *Bumbershoot, gamp, ombrifuge, rundle*—these are venerable dictionary words, all of which happen to mean "umbrella." But are they any more plausible carriers of that meaning than the non-dictionary words *rainbrella* and *dunolly*, *rainbrella* having been coined by a child and *dunolly* plucked from a map?

To this point we've mostly disported ourselves among recreational coinages. No doubt you've liked some of these more than others, but everything you've seen has been thoroughly winnowed—by me, and in many cases before me by other, uh, experts.

What do we look for in a coinage? What sets a keeper apart

177

from a discard? A number of shortcomings common to discards leap to mind.

First is what I've come to think of as the Gelett Burgess flaw: the coinage is cryptic, opaque, impenetrable. Why should *culp* (one of Burgess's words) mean "a fond delusion; an imaginary attribute"? Why should *nulkin* (another of his) mean "the core or inside history of any occurrence"? It's true that many dictionary words are of unknown origin and that many others reached their current meanings by circuitous, even bizarre, routes. In fact, Burgess's words often mimic dictionary words more accurately than sniglets or captured fugitives do. But somehow they're not as satisfying. Pretend words are more fun when they illuminate the mental processes that brought them into being.

Portmanteau words tend to have this problem licked. It's easy to figure out that *chortle* means "chuckle" and "snort," *guesstimate* is a combination of "guess" and "estimate," *Spanglish* mingles "Spanish" and "English." Sometimes, though, two old words in combination look as if they should be pronounced differently from the two words separately—and then the portmanteau word becomes impenetrable. (Because I'll be finding fault with the words that follow, I'm going to be nice and not identify their coiners.) For instance, the useful coinage *eyelie*, meaning "to pretend not to see someone," wants to be pronounced "I-lee," doesn't it? Hyphenated—"eye-lie"—it looks inauthentic. But if you try to respell it (*eyelye?*) so that readers will know how to pronounce it, the sense of where it comes from and what it means will be lost, and unpleasant images may come to mind. Discard.

Sometimes, too, a portmanteau word, like *arrowneous* ("the quality of one who drives against the arrow in a parking lot") is pronounced so much like one of the words it's derived from that it would be incomprehensible in speech. With rare exceptions, discard.

Yet other portmanteaus fall short because they have associations they shouldn't. For instance, *hozone* is supposed to mean "the place where one sock in every laundry load disappears to"—but unfortunately, nowadays the *ho* part of that suggests prostitutes as readily as hosiery.

A similar potential flaw is the intentional irrelevant allusion. Naive word coiners sometimes mistake irrelevant allusions for puns. For instance, the responses to the question I published about "going through the dirty-clothes hamper to find something clean enough to wear" included *cull-da-sack*. *Cull*, check: the word wanted has to do with culling, in the sense of selecting. *Sack*, check: the dirty clothes could just as well be in a laundry bag, or sack, as in a hamper. But what does the overall idea have to do with a cul-de-sac, or dead-end street? Uncheck. Discard.

To my mind, the least appealing irrelevant allusions are the ones that are irrelevantly naughty. You'll recall the discussion in Chapter Four about what to call an e-mail that promises but fails to include an attachment. Maybe *premature dissemination*? It's a little naughty, but at least the allusion is relevant. In contrast, re-member the search for a word that would describe "the fear of throwing a party and having no one show up"? One suggestion that came in was *premature expectulation*. Har-har. (What does the fear of throwing a party have to do with . . . ?) Suggestions made for other fugitives—never mind which ones—have included *premature gesticulation*, *premature hamperization*, and *premature detrashication*; and *somnus interruptus*, *kaputus interruptus*, *focus interruptus*, *gravitas interruptus*, *carprogress interruptus*, and *drivefastus interruptus*. Har-har-har! Similarly unappealing are irrelevant—or, heck, even relevant—allusions to Alzheimer's disease, schizophrenia, bipolar disorder, paraplegia, and so forth.

Another relatively common flaw results from a failure to think the word through and craft it well. For instance, to fit the definition "the elaborate maze of voice-mail menus and prompts encountered when phoning businesses or government offices," I like almost everything about *blabrynth*. But *labyrinth*, to which *blabrynth* is obviously meant to be related, has its "y" in the middle and an "i" in the last syllable. So shouldn't *blabrynth* be *blabberinth* or *blabyrinth*? Another example is "*petonic*, adj.: one who is embarrassed to undress in front of a household pet." OK, we get the *pet* part. But *-onic*? Is that like in *catatonic*? But that's not "embarrassed"—that's immobilized. Furthermore, is *petonic* an adjective, or does it mean "one who . . . ," in which case it's a noun? Discard.

Two other flaws I often notice are nearly each other's opposites. On the one hand, there are fugitives that no one can relate to. Suppose the definition is "not wasteful of parsnips" or "a person who sucks up to plants." Yeah? In these cases who cares how cute the coinage is. *Parsnipmonious* and *photosycophant* aren't words that anyone could conceivably want; they don't describe the world we live in. On the other hand, there are supposed fugitives for which perfectly good mainstream words already exist. For instance, "indentations on the side of a dictionary," for which *lexicaves* was coined, are in reality *thumb indexes*. "The green stuff that oozes from the center of the lobster," for which *lobsterine* was coined, is *tomalley*.

None of the above are necessarily fatal flaws, but flaws they are. If you can avoid them, your word will have a better chance of becoming an official Captured Fugitive.

* * *

And might that captured fugitive someday be domesticated and turn into a real dictionary word? This is a fond hope that many people have for their brainchildren. Alas, it is now my sad duty to dash that hope: the great majority of the words we've been discussing aren't real and never will be.

Allow me to introduce Allan Metcalf, who has a lot of experience in delivering the bad news. Since 1990, Metcalf, the executive secretary of the American Dialect Society, has overseen that organization's annual selection of "Words of the Year." It used to bother him that even though the society's members are as well informed about English as anyone anywhere, the words they choose almost invariably lack staying power. Wanting to understand why, Metcalf undertook a study. The result was his book *Predicting New Words: The Secrets of Their Success* (2002). "Successful new words," he wrote, "are alike in ways that promote their success, while unsuccessful new words are alike in ways that promote their failure."

You might imagine that the main thing successful new words would have in common is that they fill conspicuous gaps in our language. Nope. That's not true, as Metcalf explains. Even this book, *Word Fugitives*, provides a good deal of evidence against that theory. For instance, do you remember the list of words from Chapter Five that, according to Albert Morehead, English most desperately needed half a century ago? Although people have repeatedly coined words to fill most of those gaps, nothing that's been proposed has caught on. Thousands of other words have settled into English since the 1950s, but the language still lacks Morehead's fugitives.

Here's Allan Metcalf, who wrote me:

To mix a few metaphors: if a newly minted word is bright and shiny, it is almost certain to crash, burn, go up in smoke, and vanish into thin air. Whole volumes of clever new words proposed by the cleverest coiners have evaporated in this manner. Gelett Burgess, coiner of the *blurb* that remains indispensable for a book, published that word in *Burgess Unabridged*, a fully illustrated collection of 100 original coinages like *eegot*, "a selfishly interested friend, a lover of success," plus words like *eegoid* that he derived from those coinages. Except for *blurb* itself, every one of his words has failed to take root.

In the 1980s, Rich Hall published not just one but five books of sniglets. These hugely popular books contained ingenious inventions like *flirr*, "a photograph that features the camera operator's finger in the corner," and *tacangle*, "the position of one's head while biting into a taco." Of the hundreds of sniglets invented by Hall, his admirers, and his imitators, the only one that has made its way into a modicum of permanency is *sniglet* itself.

In 2001, futurologist Faith Popcorn published a much more serious collection of coinages for the new century. With Adam Hanft, she wrote a *Dictionary of the Future: The Words, Terms, and Trends That Define the Way We'll Live*. It includes words like GENE-*ology*, "the study of one's genetic history," and *atmosFear*, to describe nervousness about pollution and attacks on our air, water, and food. Although Popcorn is famous as the inventor of *cocooning*, the name for a staying-at-home trend she discerned in 1986, since then all the labels she's affixed to her predictions (right or wrong) have peeled off.

Burgess, Hall, and Popcorn are greats of word coinage, but none of them has been appreciably more successful than the most obscure amateur. High or low, notorious or anonymous, creators of clever new words have been almost uniformly frustrated in bringing them to life.

What are we to make of so many failures? It is a sad story, documented in detail in my *Predicting New Words*. In that book I discuss five qualities that allow a new word to flourish. The most important of the five is "unobtrusiveness." To become part of our standard vocabulary, a new word has to look old. Successful new words are stealth words—ones that aren't noticed until they've been with us for a while. A modern example of a stealth word (or phrase) is *heads-up*—not the long-familiar exclamation of warning, "*Heads up!*," or the adjective *heads-up* meaning "alert" or "competent," but the noun that means something like "advance information." Americans have been giving each other this kind of *heads-up* since the late twentieth century, but only now are the dictionaries beginning to recognize it. It is perfectly camouflaged in the form of its predecessors.

Even an obtrusively introduced new word can succeed if it follows a pattern that makes it appear old. The most successful conscious coinage of the twentieth century was *scofflaw*. During Prohibition, it won a $200 prize offered by a sober Harvard alumnus who wanted a word "which best expresses the idea of lawless drinker, menace, scoffer, bad citizen, or whatnot, with the biting power of *scab* or *slacker*." The winner was announced in the *Boston Herald* on January 16, 1924; today *scofflaw* is, of course, part of the standard vocabulary, and it appears in all major dictionaries.

What made *scofflaw* a success? First, it was composed of familiar ingredients—found even in the *lawless* and *scoffer* of the contest announcement. Second, combining an action verb with the object of the action is a familiar pattern in English, seen in words like *breakwater*, *makeshift*, *spitfire*, *breakfast*, and *stop-loss*.

But there's something else to be learned from *scofflaw* too. If a coined word is successful, once it enters the language, it's out of the coiner's control. *Scofflaw* was meant to shame drinkers into stopping, but instead it was adopted as enthusiastically by tipplers as by teetotalers. Two days after *scofflaw* was announced, a columnist in the *New York World* published a poem that began: "I want to be a scofflaw / And with the scofflaws stand."

By its very nature, *scofflaw* has the power not of *scab* or *slacker* but of *outlaw*, implying vigor and bravado as well as criminality. It carries no connotation of cowardice or disgust. It has nothing like the negative vibes of, say, *scumbag* or—a word of *scofflaw's* pattern—*lickspittle*. So the success of the word only provided verbal ammunition for the opponents of Prohibition and may even have helped bring about Prohibition's demise a decade later.

That is the sad lesson for would-be coiners of words: damned if you succeed, damned if you don't. It doesn't mean you have to stop trying, though. I sneaked a new coinage of my own into the preceding paragraphs somewhere. If you can't find it, it might succeed.

★ ★ ★

So there you have it. Is this bad news for people who coin words for fun? No doubt it will come as a blow to anyone who believes in elves and Tinker Bell. It may also upset the kind of person who, having won a game of Monopoly, is disappointed that the real estate and the money aren't real and theirs to keep. (What would we call someone like that? Surely such a person is too rare to deserve a name.) Not without reason have we called what's been happening in this book recreational word coining. And by the way, if you're still wondering what Metcalf's coinage was, it's *stealth word*.

Please also bear in mind that there are people we might be proud to know—language lovers and language professionals, even—who don't share the pleasure we take in recreational word coining. In fact, let's hear from a couple of them.

RUSTLED UP

John E. McIntyre, the copy chief at *The Baltimore Sun* and the past president of the American Copy Editors Society, wrote me:

As a copy editor and enforcer of my paper's style rules, I don't have much truck with coining or redefining words; rather, I look at jocularities and vogue words with a suspicious eye, resisting them until they lodge in the language.

Besides that, as a sometime English major, I am more given to excavating obsolete or exotic words and expressions from their context. "Is everything going *tickety-boo*?" I sometimes ask colleagues on the copy desk. If they haven't read Wodehouse, God knows what they imagine I'm saying.

Sockdolager and its variants (from *sock*, "a punch," and *doxology*), to mean "a final and conclusive blow," have crept into my work routine. When the night's work is done, my Nunc Dimittis to the copy desk is "Well, I guess I know enough, old gal, to turn you inside out, you sockdologizing old mantrap." (That line from *Our American Cousin* was the last human speech Abraham Lincoln heard in this life.) "We've been *sockdologized*," the copy editors chortle as they store their belongings and flee into the night.

What's more, I'm an old guy, in my fifties. Instead of waiting for the tides to cast new words onto the strand, I dig away in the sand for bright little fragments of the language from an earlier time. Young people like novelty, and they are better equipped to enjoy it.

And the humorist P. J. O'Rourke wrote me:

I do use words that aren't in dictionaries, but only at work. That is, when I'm on the job as a humorist, trying to be funny, I employ puns, wordplay, coinages, and any other instruments of linguistic clowning that come to hand. But I'm not good with these tools. The only word I've ever invented that I like is *Smug-wump*—a person who doesn't know what to think politically but is very self-satisfied with thinking it.

The truth is that I'm a language Platonist. The words I think are mere shadows on the cave wall of my mind. Somewhere there are perfect words that mean exactly what I'm trying to mean. My Platonic ideal is a couple hundred pounds of *Oxford English Dictionary*, where I waste whole days teasing out the exact shade of definition I seek—for example, between *ossified* and *osseous*.

I know I'm wrong. For one thing, I can't stand Plato as a philosopher. And communication is social science, not math. But something in me (a latent autism, perhaps) makes me wish words had positions on an X-Y axis instead of customary (not to mention novel) usages.

★ ★ ★

Ah, well. John McIntyre and P. J. O'Rourke are certainly entitled to their opinions. Not everyone likes to play Monopoly, either. It *is* all a game, and here's hoping you've enjoyed it.

But let's have one more fugitive, as a last hurrah:

"Shouldn't there be an expression for the feeling you get when you finish reading a book you don't want to ever end?"
—Barry Cranmer, Mount Laurel, N.J.

BIBLIOGRAPHY

Mostly recreationally coined words; sources given in chronological order:

"Improvised Words," an unsigned article in the "Contributors' Club" section of *The Atlantic Monthly*, November 1908.

Burgess Unabridged: A Dictionary of Words You Have Always Needed, by Gelett Burgess, Frederick A. Stokes Company, 1914.

"A Volley of Words," by Lewis Burke Frumkes, in the December 1976 issue of *Harper's Magazine*. This lexicon of words from *abdolatry* to *zonoobia*, all coined by Frumkes, was reprinted in *How to Raise Your I.Q. by Eating Gifted Children*, a collection of humorous essays by Frumkes, McGraw-Hill, 1979.

Brave New Words, by Bill Sherk, Doubleday Canada and Alger Press, 1979.

More Brave New Words, by Bill Sherk, Doubleday Canada and Doubleday, 1981.

"*Mad*'s New Phobias for the '80's," by John Ficarra, *Mad* magazine, March 1981.

The Meaning of Liff, by Douglas Adams and John Lloyd, Pan Books and Faber & Faber, 1983.

Not the Webster's Dictionary, by Byron Preiss and Michael Sorkin, Wallaby Books, 1983.

BIBLIOGRAPHY

Bob Levey's Washington, a now-retired column in *The Washington Post*, included a monthly neologism contest from 1983 to 2003.

Sniglets, by Rich Hall and Friends, Collier Books, 1984.

More Sniglets, by Rich Hall and Friends, Collier Books, 1985.

Unexplained Sniglets of the Universe, by Rich Hall and Friends, Collier Books, 1986.

Angry Young Sniglets, by Rich Hall and Friends, Collier Books, 1987.

When Sniglets Ruled the Earth, by Rich Hall, Collier Books, 1989.

The Deeper Meaning of Liff, by Douglas Adams and John Lloyd, Pan Books and Faber & Faber, 1992.

In a Word: A Dictionary of Words That Don't Exist, But Ought To, edited by Jack Hitt, Laurel, 1992.

An Exaltation of Larks: The Ultimate Edition, by James Lipton, Penguin, 1993. The first edition of this book was published by Grossman in 1968.

Family Words: The Dictionary for People Who Don't Know a Frone from a Brinkle, by Paul Dickson, Broadcast Interview Source, 1998.

"Word Fugitives: America's 10 Most Wanted Words," Atlantic Unbound, www.theatlantic.com/unbound/fugitives, active 1998–1999.

Wanted Words: From Amalgamots to Undercarments, edited by Jane Farrow, Stoddart Publishing, 2000.

Wanted Words 2: From Armajello to Yawncore, edited by Jane Farrow, Stoddart Publishing, 2001.

Word Ways: The Journal of Recreational Linguistics, now edited by Ross Eckler, 1968–present. To see a sample of articles from the magazine or to subscribe, visit www.wordways.com.

The Style Invitational contest, *The Washington Post*, by Gene Weingarten, 1993–2003, and Pat Myers, 2003–present. Current and recent contests can be found at www.washingtonpost.com; type *style invitational* into the site's search bar.

Word Court, a syndicated weekly newspaper column by Barbara Wallraff, occasionally discusses neologisms. Its archives, from 2003 to the present, can be found at www.wordcourt.com.

Mostly dictionary words (past, present, and future); sources given in alphabetical order by title:

DailyCandy, an e-mail newsletter and Web site edited by Dany Levy, at www.dailycandy.com. To find the archives of "chick-speak," visit the site and search for *lexicon*.

The Devil's Dictionary, by Ambrose Bierce, Oxford, 1999.

Diagnostic and Statistical Manual of Mental Disorders, fourth edition, by the American Psychiatric Association, 1994.

The Disheveled Dictionary: A Curious Caper through Our Sumptuous Lexicon, by Karen Elizabeth Gordon, Houghton Mifflin, 1997.

Forgotten English, by Jeffrey Kacirk, Quill, 1997.

More Weird and Wonderful Words, edited by Erin McKean, Oxford, 2003.

Oxford English Dictionary Online, Oxford, at dictionary.oed.com.

Predicting New Words: The Secrets of Their Success, by Allan Metcalf, Houghton Mifflin, 2002.

There's a Word for It! A Grandiloquent Guide to Life, by Charles Harrington Elster, Scribner, 1996.

They Have a Word For It: A Lighthearted Lexicon of Untranslatable Words and Phrases, by Howard Rheingold, Jeremy P. Tarcher, 1988.

Weird and Wonderful Words, edited by Erin McKean, Oxford, 2003.

The Word Museum: The Most Remarkable English Ever Forgotten, by Jeffrey Kacirk, Touchstone, 2000.

Words: A Connoisseur's Collection of Old and New, Weird and Wonderful, Useful and Outlandish Words, by Paul Dickson, Delacorte, 1982.

Word Spy: The Word Lover's Guide to Modern Culture, by Paul McFedries,

Broadway Books, 2004. A related Web site, The Word Spy, can be found at www.wordspy.com.

World Wide Words, a weekly e-mail newsletter and Web site by Michael Quinion, at www.worldwidewords.org.

Xenia: A Hoard of Lost Words, Eighteenth-Century Street Lingo, and a Few Completely Confabulated Terms Collected and Exemplified, by Coleman Barks, Maypop, 1994.